LET
Stacy Lee
GEORGE
DO IT!

A Political & Spiritual Awakening!

STACY LEE GEORGE

authorHOUSE®

AuthorHouse™
1663 Liberty Drive
Bloomington, IN 47403
www.authorhouse.com
Phone: 833-262-8899

Published by AuthorHouse 09/21/2021

ISBN: 978-1-6655-3839-8 (sc)
ISBN: 978-1-6655-3837-4 (hc)
ISBN: 978-1-6655-3838-1 (e)

Library of Congress Control Number: 2021919153

Print information available on the last page.

DEDICATION

This book is dedicated to the God of Israel (my GOD) and His people who are called by His name. Injustice, unfairness, and corruption are not of GOD; through the words of this book that was inspired by the Holy Spirit, eyes will be opened shedding light on unethical government operations. This will cause satan to lose a part of his kingdom on earth every time this book is read and understood.

Hosea 4:6 KJV

6 My people are destroyed for lack of knowledge:

Luke 4:5-7 NKJV

5 Then the devil, taking Him (Jesus) up on a high mountain,
showed Him all the kingdoms of the world in a moment
of time. 6 And the devil said to Him, "All this authority I
will give You, and their glory; for this has been delivered
to me, and I give it to whomever I wish. 7 Therefore,
if You will worship before me, all will be Yours."

CONTENTS

THIS TESTIMONY IS TRUE, AND I GIVE IT TO YOU!

If I had a testimony, what would it be?
It would be lessons I have learned pay attention and you will see;

A testimony, I find it hard to tell,
It's like your favorite treasure you don't want to sell;

It comes straight from my heart, and it humbles my pride to discuss,
GOD put it on my heart to tell you, so I am not going to put up a fuss;

There are only four things in life you can really do,
Think about this closely and you will know it's true.

I have done the right thing for the right reason,
This happened a lot, but it had its season;

I have done the right thing for the wrong reason,
This happened sometimes but just for a season;

I have done the wrong thing for the right reason,
This happened at times, but this was just another season;

But NEVER do the wrong thing for the wrong reason!
For this there is no season;

I will start with a story as a small child,
I would have buckteeth in the front and blond hair running wild;

I would be shy as I could be,
I would cover my face and peep between my fingers to see;

I remember this kid well, it was me and I was twelve,
An adult I would become as I put my toys on the shelve;

A boy no more and I would look for a job,
I would cry with anger then self-pity would turn it to a sob;

What happened? What could it be?
My Dad was trimming limbs for a neighbor when he fell from a tree;

He was paralyzed for the rest of his life,
This would begin a life of struggle and strife;

It wasn't all bad just watch and see,
It brought our family close, and for a season that's the way it would be;

Next, I would get braces to fix those buck teeth in my mouth,
The dentist said, "Keep that brace in at night, tighten it too, or this whole thing will go south;"

In the eleventh grade I lost my shyness and started to talk,
It was almost like crawling as a baby and then suddenly you walk;

Let's jump through time when GOD would change my life,
The devil had taken over and I would lose my first wife;

Bad decisions I would make, and it would cost me a lot,
You would think I would learn, but for a while I would not;
I was 23 when I gave into a tug at my heart,
I would go to the alter, hit my knees, confess my sins, and ask my savior for a new start;

I would go to church for a while and then in a night club I would be,
I would fall in the devil's trap, but eventually I would see;

I would love to tell you a fairy tale and make you believe it was true,
I would tell you in life a storm will not come, and the sky will always be blue;

That would be a lie so I will shoot straight to the point,
GOD has a job for you, and he is wanting to anoint;

I did not tell you earlier, but I will tell you now,
I did the wrong thing for the wrong reason, and I will give you examples of how;

I made idols of things; things you might not think of,
Let's start with dove season in September; through hell or high water I was going to shoot me a dove;

My Grandma Rada fell sick with cancer, and it took her life in just days,
Me, I was in a dove field when she would die; I knew I was wrong, and I needed to change my ways;

My Grandma May would die a slow death, but similar I would be,
We would have her funeral and I would almost be late because I was deer hunting in a tree;

Are you seeing this picture I am painting for you?
If you see yourself in that mirror, it's time to sit on that pew;

When I started this poem, I didn't know where it would go,
The Holy Ghost took over and he put on a show;

I have told you a lot; but GOD says, "it is time to close up the shop."
GOD says, "With all the bad things I have done it's time for a cleaning so I will get you a mop."

The bucket is full of dirty water, and I made a mess,
GOD gave me a blood-stained mop and what comes, next I will let you guess;

He said, "Keep this mop for the rest of your days on earth."
"I save a mop for everyone, and I stash it back at your birth."

The blood stain is from Jesus because he saved your soul,
Don't wander around lost mopping your mess; make finding Jesus your goal;

Don't do as I have done do as I say,
Get your Bible, Stay in GOD's word and you will not go astray!

My personal testimony in the form of a Poem by Stacy Lee George

Psalm 118:5-7 KJV

I called upon the LORD in distress: The LORD answered me and set me in a large place. The LORD is on my side; I will not fear: What can man do unto me? The LORD taketh my part with them that help me: Therefore shall I see my desire upon them that hate me.

FOREWORD BY DUANE C. WOODALL

There is a 'Mayberry like' quality inherent within 'Let Stacy Lee George Do It' which is refreshing and at the same time necessary. It's that moment when Andy Taylor shakes his head at the town's mayor saying, "Mr. Mayor, you can't do that". There is no ill will on the sheriff's part directed toward the mayor, just a common man's inner knowing regarding 'doing the right thing'.

Stacy's simple autobiographical account is intended to show the everyday person the route he used to make a difference and suggest why someone making this difference is so important. It is my belief if more individuals had in the past held those in positions of authority to a higher standard, we would not be faced with the results we see today.

By doing nothing and allowing travesties to go unchecked a false sense of security exists within those in positions of power whereby because they have gotten away with so much for so long, it is believed by them they can now 'get away with anything' unchecked, that their bluff never be called and that their injustices will never be brought to light.

Stacy's book shows he has 'done it' it still can be done, it's not too late and if we give him the opportunity it's still not too late to 'Let Stacy Let George Do it'.

I can state from my firsthand knowledge, because I have known Stacy his entire life, that his intentions are earnest, he is the living personification of Mayberry's Andy, who still personally likes the town's mayor but cannot in all good conscience, sit back and allow him to do the wrong thing.

It seems we have arrived at a point, because for decades we have 'looked the other way' as our authority figures made the wrong moral and often illegal decisions, that we are now in a world created by our own 'looking the other way' and as a result of our refusal to bring any wrong doing to the forefront and into the light we are in a world where our leadership thinks they can now 'do anything'.

Stacy's book exists as a beacon to us all saying: "Look, this can be done, I did it, here is how, you can accomplish this too."

His simple writing here, which begins with him stating his method, then onto the ways he used the foundational laws already in existence to remedy wrongful actions is now very relevant.

There is a no more pertinent time than now to give Stacy's written account of and experienced remedy to a world in need. This book is for anyone who has felt helpless as to 'What to do'. You need look no further. What can be done exists within the words of this eye-opening book, 'Let Stacy Lee George Do It'.

Duane C. Woodall
August 13, 2021

A POLITICAL AWAKENING (GEORGE STYLE)

A heavenly cleansing for some, but pure Hell on Earth to others; it all depends on who you ask. In 1997 politics was injected into my body like a flu vaccine, but there was a problem. The virus now inside me was far from being dead; it was very much alive. As I fought fiercely against this political virus it consumed me like a fiery furnace. The fire still burns.

I was twenty-nine years young, not old, with much to learn about courthouse politics in Morgan County, Alabama. The Morgan County mafia was alive and well in Decatur, Alabama (the county seat). As I tell you this true story the hair on the back of my neck stands up. I always had a dream as a child of living in a small house with a few acres of land. My family had always lived in rental houses and later in life we were blessed with a mobile home. We would eventually own this home. At the time this political awakening started to unfold I was living in my late grandmother's 1968 mobile home on an acre of land she left me when she passed on. My income level was finally where it needed to be, and I was ready to build my house. The land I thought I would someday own was being paid for through owner finance.

I had been clearing brush for a couple of years on the property. The original survey cost was just less than two thousand dollars; I had spent one week of my vacation time assisting surveyors to keep the surveying cost down. There was also a property line dispute over a portion of the land, and this caused me great grief.

As I started hauling rock to the narrow road the property was on a huge problem presented itself to me. This property was not located on a county-maintained road. Subdivision rules had been adopted by the county commission in Morgan County by recommendation of the county engineer a few years earlier. I learned something the hard way and so did the Morgan County Commission at the time. This road that ran through multiple landowners was not a county-maintained road. There are basically three types of roads: county-maintained roads, private drives, and public roads.

To cut a long story short, I was forced to sell my property back to the original landowner because the road was public, but not county maintained. The county commission would not approve the sale of the property. This was scary that the government could stop someone from buying and selling land in the rural areas of a county. I was blessed by the fact the original property owner gave me my money back except for the surveying fee. I was mad then and although time has passed, I still feel the fire burning inside.

During this time my great grandmother Margie F. Holmes (November 27, 1902, until June 1, 1997) passed away. Former Governor Guy Hunt was her pastor at the Gumpond Primitive Baptist Church, and he said a few words at her graveside service. In addition, former Governor Hunt was the Cullman County Probate Judge who performed the marriage ceremony for my mom and dad in 1968. The day of my great grandmother's funeral my heart felt as if someone was pulling it from my chest. The day before it felt the same way as I dug her grave by hand with very little help (I just did not ask for any help) going 6 feet deep not 4 feet because without a vault you must go 6 feet deep. As I fought the urge to speak to former Governor Guy Hunt the Holy Spirit was tugging at me and thick sweat was draining down my face like melting lava from a volcano. Finally, I gave in, and I said, "Guy, I need to talk to you sometime." Guy replied, "Come by anytime. Helen and I are usually around the house."

My impatient attitude and high energy took little time to go visit the Hunt family home. I remember that day with detail almost as well as what I was doing on September 11, 2001, when terrorism on the home front become real. My nerves were tingling all over my body and the hair on the back of my neck was electrically charged, as if I was jumping on a trampoline during a cold winter's day preparing to touch metal discharging spiritual static energy. It was the Holy Spirit, and I did not know it. I knocked on the door and Guy opened the door with a smile. He said, "let us go for a walk." We walked through a small orchard as I remember. I said, "Guy, something is pulling on my heart about politics, and I feel led to run for governor one day." Guy simply said, "If you plan to run for governor you need to start finding good honest people to put around you right now." He looked sternly and said, "First, find you a county commission seat in Morgan County to run for." As I left his humble home, I felt a sense of calmness similar to the night I was baptized.

I registered to vote the next week quickly joining the Republican Party in Morgan County. I then registered nearly 300 new voters in a three-year campaign crusade to be the first Republican County Commissioner elected in Morgan County since Reconstruction. In Morgan County at the time all commissioners run at-large; this means everyone in Morgan County including all cities vote in this election. Roughly sixty-thousand registered voters have an opportunity to vote in this election. With no Republican primary opposition, I could concentrate on the rather popular Democrat County commissioner that had already served 12 years. Not one person thought I could win with nearly zero money. I spent a lot of time meeting people over the next 3 years. Now, the picture becomes clear; the same county commission that denied me the ability to buy land in Morgan County would feel my full wrath. The fire is still burning inside me.

I won on my first run for political office by 78 votes out of 39,500 cast that day in November of 2000. I received the largest Black American vote since reconstruction. I received more votes than any other Republican throughout printed history in Morgan County at the Benjamin Davis voting precinct in Northwest Decatur, Alabama. By the grace of GOD, I won, but what was unleashed on Morgan County some could only call "pure Hell". As you look through many of the articles by various newspapers you can draw your own conclusion. Was it Heaven or Hell in Morgan County? The answer is simple; it depends on who you ask. Actions speak better than words, but these actions had consequences and every person the corruption web would touch bled red blood for eight years in Morgan County; I did my share of bleeding too. Some of the elected politicians survived defeat by coming out of the darkness of deception. Some politicians refused to change, and they were consumed in the political firestorm.

Daniel 7:10

A stream of fire issued
and came out from before him;
a thousand thousands served him,
and ten thousand times ten thousand stood before him;
the court sat in judgment,
and the books were opened.

Hartselle gridlock?

News as local will be crowding, but traffic snarls may worsen.

RIVERFRONT B1

COLLEGE SCOREBOARD

Mississippi State	29	Florida	41	So. Mississippi	33
Alabama	7	South Carolina	21	UAB (2OT)	30
Tennessee	63	Auburn	28	Alabama A&M	27
Arkansas	20	Georgia (OT)	26	Alcorn State	20
Vanderbilt	24	LSU	20	UNA	21
Kentucky	20	Ole Miss	9	West Alabama	14

Gala XVI honorees

Educator Penelope Banks and Dr. Jack Bennett profiled.

LIVING E1

THE DECATUR DAILY

Morgan's 1st GOP commissioner

Stacy George worked entire county looking for new supporters

Stacy George will be sworn in as Morgan County's newest commissioner Monday.

AREA DEATHS

THE WEATHER

WHAT'S INSIDE?

CHECK OUT THE INTERACTIVE FEATURES OF THE DAILY'S ONLINE EDITION AT www.decaturdaily.com

George

Continued from page A1

Subdivision Rules (County)

- The reason I registered to vote in 1997.
- The Morgan County Commission used these rules to deny me the right to buy land in rural Morgan County.
- I decided to run for Commissioner and won my first run in 2000.
- This was all caused by a government mandate.

Subdivision Rules for rural Morgan County.

(See Sample Certificate - Appendix E) It is advisable that the property owner have a land survey made of the property in question and that the surveyor's certificate be attached to and become a part of the Certificate to Subdivide. The property owner shall submit the original and two copies of the Certificate to Subdivide to the County Engineer with a letter from the owner requesting approval by the County Commission.

b) The County Commission will review the request as to its conformity with the Subdivision Standards.

c) The County Commission will approve, approve on condition, or deny approval of said Certificate to Subdivide. If approved, the Certificate shall be signed and acknowledged by the Chairman of the Morgan County Commission and notarized.

d) The County Commission shall return the original of the Certificate to Subdivide to the property owner or his representative.

e) The property owner or his representative shall have the approved original of the Certificate to Subdivide recorded in the Office of the Judge of Probate of Morgan County.

SECTION NINE - SEVERABILITY AND SEPARABILITY

Should any article, section, subsection, or provision of these Subdivision Standards be declared by a court of competent jurisdiction to be invalid or unconstitutional, such decision shall not affect the validity or constitutionality of these Subdivision Standards as a whole or any part thereof other than the part so declared to be invalid or unconstitutional.

SECTION TEN - EFFECTIVE DATE

These Subdivision Standards shall take effect and be in force from and after the date of adoption.

ADOPTED THIS THE 11th DAY OF February, 1985.

MORGAN COUNTY COMMISSION OF
MORGAN COUNTY, ALABAMA

By: [signature]
Larry Bennich, Chairman

ATTEST:

[signature]

1968 Probate Judge Guy Hunt

Mom   Dad

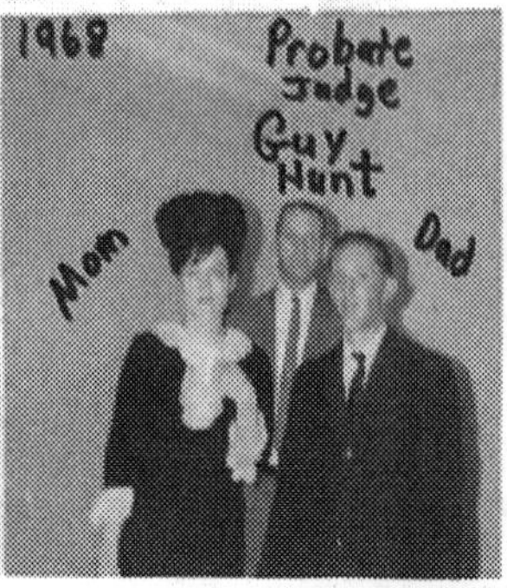

Guy Hunt
Governor
Republican

Grandma Rada
Grandpa Dison
Me / inside 1968 model
mobile home.

RE-ELECT
LET
GEORGE
DO IT
MORGAN CO. COMM. D1

Guy Hunt Governor.

JESUS CHRIST
IS THE ✝ ANSWER
Jesus Christ is the Answer

Grandma
Rada

Sister Kristie

Actual post hole diggers
used to dig my
Great Grandmother's grave
(Margie F. Holmes)

TUESDAY, JULY 10, 2001
THE DECATUR DAILY

Morgan commission rejects George's bid for voting by district

By Sheryl Marsh
DAILY Staff Writer

The Decatur Daily wednesday Nov. 8, 2000

Morgan

Continued from page B1

George grabs Morgan upset

▶ Republican Stacy Lee George's narrow win against Democratic incumbent Howard Jenkins shocked Morgan County Commission members. In complete but unofficial results, George won by 78 votes, B1
▶ More election coverage, A5, A8, B2, B4

The Decatur Daily
Courtesy of Sheryl Marsh

Morgan Co. Commission

Courtesy of The Decatur Daily
writer Sheryl Marsh

George
Continued from page C1

Lawmakers unwilling to change Morgan at-large voting districts

By Clay Redden
DAILY Staff Writer

MONTGOMERY — A petition drive to change the way Morgan County Commission members are elected isn't getting support from state lawmakers.

HARTSELLE ENQUIRER

Thursday, March 2, 2000 — Two Sections, 50 Cents

Petition promotes voting by districts

Legislative delegation asked to let voters decide the issue

By Cil Knight
Hartselle Enquirer

Stacy George, a political activist who lives in the Ryan Community has petitioned Morgan County's Legislative delegation for the second time in two years to sponsor a bill to let Morgan County voters decide the issue of at-large or district-only voting for county commissioners.

George, 31, a Republican, said he placed a petition bearing the signatures of 1,080 qualified Morgan County voters in the hands of Rep. Jeremy Oden (Rep.) on February 21. It proposes for consideration an amendment which reads as follows: "The qualified electors of each district shall elect their own county commissioner in their county district in which the commissioner already must be a resident."

George said the petition was launched in March 1999 and bears the signatures of a broad cross section of voters from Trinity to Morgan City. "I've found everywhere I've been that the people want the opportunity to elect their own district commissioner. But that won't happen until our legislative delegation agrees to let the issue be brought forward and put to a vote. I would like to see this included on the ballot at the next general election in November," he pointed out.

George said he circulated a similar petition in 1998 and was able to get it signed by 1,000 voters. However, it got stuck in the hands of the legislative delegation and a local bill calling for an election was not introduced. "I feel better about the chances that something positive will happen this time," George stated. "This is an issue that's not going away. Interest

Stacey George

among the voters is high and I feel our representatives are aware of that."

George pointed out that prior to 1973 Morgan County's commissioners were elected by districts and in all but 14 of Alabama's 67 counties they are elected in that manner today.

He used the following example

Please see PETITION, Page A-5

Saturday, Jan. 31, 2004

Codes in Morgan don't sit too well

By CHARLES WHISENANT
The Arab Tribune

"Not just no, but hell no ..."

That was Tex Byess' response when asked if he favors proposed building codes in Morgan County.

"If it served a real purpose I might be for it," Byess said. "But the only purpose it will serve is to cost me and everyone else money."

The Morgan County Commission is looking into adopting building codes for the rural parts of the county. Among other regulations, the codes would require residents to buy a permit from the county before building a house, an addition to a house, shed and many other projects.

Though expressed somewhat differently, Tommy Griffin, Leon Mooney, District 4 Commissioner Stacy George and 300 petition signers agree with Byess and want the building codes idea thrown out like construction scrap wood.

Some members of the commission asked county attorney Bill Shinn to research building codes. Shinn later reported to the commission that it had the authority to enforce laws and hire building inspectors.

The commission seems to be split 3-2 in favor of the codes. Chairman Larry Bennich and commissioners Don Stisher and Jeff Clark, all Democrats, are in favor while Republican Commissioners Stacy George and John Glasscock are against the proposal.

"We have plenty of rules and regulations in place now with subdivision rules that are enforced and flood ordinances that are enforced," George said. "The idea would be just another bureaucracy in Morgan County – another tax

Please see BUILDING, Page 2

THE DECATUR DAILY, Sunday morning, April 25, 1999

Some residents want commission vote by districts

By Sheryl Marsh
DAILY Staff Writer

A Ryan resident is on a mission to take Morgan County back to its former way of electing county commissioners.

Stacy George, 30, said he feels the county should elect commissioners by district vote rather than at large.

George is on a campaign to get that done and has a petition bearing the names of more than 700 signatures of county residents whom he says share the same belief.

"My reason for doing this is to assure the people in each district full representation of their needs and direct interests," he said.

He also said he's considering running for office. He resides in District 4.

Larry Bennich
Commission chairman

"The way it is at this time people have representation from four members and a chairman and all of us are responsible for their needs. Each commissioner represents every person in Morgan County. The commissioners spend people's money from all over the county, not just one district," he said.

At large better?

"If we had district voting and you have a problem with a commissioner because he doesn't spend money in your district, but in the one he represents, you can't do anything about it because you can't vote on him," said Bennich.

District 1 commissioner Jeff Clark said he understands both voting methods, but he feels at-large is better.

"My personal opinion is that it would hurt the county, but I can see where it would appeal to the citizens to go to a district vote. It would be similar to the way it is in other counties to have district voting," he said.

"If that would happen and I run for my district, I would have no reason to listen to voters in other districts because I feel like it wouldn't pertain to me."

Getting law changed

George said he'd rather avoid putting the matter to a vote, so he plans to first present the petition to the local legislative delegation.

Morgan County Probate Judge Bobby Day said there's nothing in election laws that allows for a person to try to change the way public officials are elected by presenting a petition.

"It's my opinion that he would have to get that law changed through the local legislative body," Day said.

George initially said he was told he needed 1 percent of registered voters to get the issue on a ballot, but said he later found out he needed to lobby the local legislators to get them to change the law.

"I plan to meet with them and show them the number of voters in the county who want to go back to district voting. I will ask them to draft an amendment to the bill to change it back to district voting," George said.

He said he has 700 signatures and there are copies of the petition still circulating.

The county has 60,300 voters, according to the Board of Registrars.

Echoes comments

District 4 Commissioner Howard Jenkins comments were basically the same.

"I think if we go back to the way we were we'll be backing up as far as the way we serve the people of Morgan County because now other commissioners care what's going on. They have to have the vote in all districts. If it was district voting they would be focused on their one particular district," Jenkins said.

District 3 Commissioner Don Stisher said he believes the current method is the most fair because it leaves commissioners accountable for the entire county.

"Our focus is on working together in unity and I think if we were to separate that, it would slow our efforts on a lot of projects, such as industrial development. All the chambers of commerce are merging and we're all working together and by doing so we can have good accomplishments."

Both Limestone and Lawrence counties have district voting.

Changed in 1973

Day said members of the commission were elected by districts until 1973 when then-Sen. Bob Harris sponsored a bill to change to at-large voting. The law requires that each member lives in the district he represents.

Day said before the law could be changed, it would have to be approved by the U.S. Justice Department because of the 1965 Voting Rights Act.

Commission Chairman Larry Bennich and members oppose district voting.

March 2, 2000 HARTSELLE ENQUIRER A-5

Petition

Continued from A-1

to illustrate the impact the change ... itself" ... on the outcome of the 1996 election in his district.

Robert Abercrombie (District 4 commissioner) won the 1972 election over his opponent by a greater than two-to-one margin. In 1973, Morgan County changed to at-large voting. Subsequently, he was defeated in a run-off in the 1976 election even though he received more than 50 per cent of the vote in District #4 in a three-man race and out-polled his opponent among district voters in the

"That was the beginning of the bureaucracy of non-representation in our county," George said. "Abercrombie was beaten in the county as a whole but not by the people in his own district. I'm sure the people of District #4 felt like they were robbed because the man who they felt would best represent them lost the election."

"Since the effort was begun to change the commission election process, the rural areas of Morgan County have gotten more new bridges, handrails and resurfaced roads than ever before," George stated. "I'm thankful for that but it doesn't solve the problem we've had for 25 years. Our children's generation must not suffer the same as we have, and eventually at-large voting will be changed back to district-only voting. I only wish the current legislative delegation would allow us to vote on this issue so it can be put to rest one way or the other."

Building

Continued from Page 1

that the taxpayers would be stuck with. It's just another tax they are trying to pass."

George said the county has good, qualified contractors who know what they are doing, and if residents want someone to inspect their building, they can hire someone.

Bennich and Stisher have said building codes would be a "protective shield for residents."

George said that while he is opposed to building codes, he would be in favor of putting the question on a ballot and letting the people decide.

"Take it out of the hands of the commission and let the people decide if they want it," he said. "I just won't vote for something that I know most people are against."

Tony Taylor, a resident of Eva, presented the commission Monday with a petition that contains more than 300 names against building codes.

Griffin, a Morgan City contractor, said Thursday that he and other builders have enough trouble out of Morgan County's engineer without adding a building inspector.

"This is terrible," Griffin said. "It will create problems, because you won't be able to find a building inspector, and when you do, he'll get to your site when he feels like it. It'll delay us and cost us a lot of money."

Griffin said the commission does what it can to create more chaos for the citizens every chance it gets.

"We have problems with (Bennich)," he said. "We get nothing from Decatur but a tax bill. We have a break-in or a theft, and they'll send a deputy to take a report, but they never follow up."

Leon Mooney of Hulaco is also opposed to building codes.

"I don't have a whole lot of information about it yet, but what I have heard I don't like," Mooney said.

Tex Byess, owner of Morgan City Feed and Seed, said he doesn't want codes or inspectors.

"If they pass it they'll have to hire more people, then if you want to build something you'll have to wait on them to come inspect it, and they'll do that when they get good and ready."

Byess said it amounts to a violation of his privacy.

"If I wanted to go by a bunch of rules and regulations, I'd move to town," he said. "The reason I live in the county is I like the freedom."

Byess said he has one idea that would rule out building codes for him – because Marshall County doesn't have building codes.

"I'd like to see everyone on (Brindlee) mountain, who lives in Morgan County, be annexed in to Marshall County," he said. "We don't get anything out of Decatur.

"We get our water from Marshall County (Arab Water Works), our lights from Marshall County (Arab Electric Cooperative), our phone from Marshall County (Brindlee Mountain Telephone Co.). We might as well be in Marshall County."

Byess said that all of the tax money that comes into Morgan County goes to Bennich and "his buddies in and around Decatur."

"Decatur has a say in who commissioner is here in Morgan City and that's not right," he said. "It's always been that way. We're totally ignored by the county."

Morgan County elects commissioners at large and not by districts.

WHO IS STACY LEE GEORGE?

I would describe myself as a person who fears only GOD. A man who believes GOD makes no mistakes and every person has a purpose in life. Not many of us find that purpose because GOD's plan is not the easiest path. GOD directs our path. Now, follow me as I describe the Holy Spirit steering my path. I was created in the spring of 1968 and born 9 months later in Arab, Alabama January 12, 1969. As young as I can remember I always hunted pretty much year around. My dad had one rule and it was simple. If you kill "it" you eat it except for an opossum, a black bird, or a crow. I did my share of eating blue jay birds, red birds, red robin birds, and everything in between.

I was raised in the Ryan community in eastern Morgan County, Alabama. The Ryan community is located at the foothills of the Appalachian Mountains. Generations attended the Ryan School, the old building, built of stone and still standing at the top of Ryan Mountain. This location is just south of Huntsville, east of Decatur, and just west of Arab where I currently live.

On my mom's side of the family I have fewer memories, but my Grandpa Thomas Lee May (November 7, 1897, until January 6, 1977) was a unique character. I was named after my Grandpa May and people simply called him Lee. I remember chickens and hogs best including a dose of some homebrew one time. That homebrew (homemade beer) I remember was so sweet tasting, but it was a done deal when my mama Leola May George found out. I remember he was not much interested with anybody dealing with the government being on our property. He was known to do a lot of chicken fighting back in the day.

My only tie to politics at all comes from my mother's side. I have some data from the family tree, but my great Grandpa May was the first Judge of Marshall County years ago. I am not sure how many times you put great in front of grandpa, but you get the picture. I found this out when some of the May descendants researched the family tree finding out my Great Grandpa May down the descendant line had been deemed incompetent and he was taken out of the May family will. This resulted in my mom being raised extremely poor, but the cousins did quite well. The May family owned a large part of Marshall County and my mom's rather wealthy cousins still do. You see in those days I understand a lot of people were cut out of wills in the same manner. There was greed then and there is greed now. Throughout the King James Bible there has always been greed and there always will be.

On my dad's side of the family Henry Charles "Snooks" George (March 16, 1941, until January 30, 2011) I have my most vivid memories of my dad's mom grandma Rada (Holmes) George Sheppard (November 17, 1918, until September 15, 1990) was the glue that held our family together. She always had a Sunday meal, and everyone always participated. The meal ranged from golden brown fried chicken to some fresh caught Crappie fish. I always loved to eat those crispy fish tails.

Politics was simple, and she was a Democrat until the day she died. My Grandma Rada's parents, Henry E. Holmes (October 1, 1893, until December 22, 1981) and Margie F. Holmes (November 27, 1902, until June 1, 1997) were the parents of nearly a dozen children. For most of their lives Maw maw and Paw paw had an outhouse, pulled well water by a pail, and heated with an iron stove. I'm sure grandma had to be overwhelmed with so many children. I only knew a sweet gentle and kind soul, who loved seeing her grandchildren.

Grandma had only kindness for all. Margie F. Holmes attended the Gum Pond Primitive Baptist Church. The pastor every other Sunday was Guy Hunt from nearby Holly Pond, and he also happened to be a Republican Probate Judge in Cullman County. At that time being a Republican elected official was very rare. He ran as a Republican for Governor at a time when the current democrat candidates were slinging mud at each other at levels escalating even for Alabamians. The voters had enough and with the tides of change moving in the Republican favor for Guy Hunt. He was the pastor of my grandmother's small church. Guy became the first Republican Governor since reconstruction. It's still a quaint special place up a winding mountain road from the Ryan Community of my youth. It never left my mind that a Cullman County Probate Judge and a pastor, a man I knew as wise, and caring could make such a difference. It proved to me the winds of change (in a political sense) could blow all different ways. This gusty wind carried some to great heights and some to great lows.

The best I can remember in first grade I began to discern between right and wrong, although I still did my share of wrong. One thing in my life that was consistent is the heartfelt feeling of fairness. Think about it, "Whether something is done right or wrong is irrelevant when it comes to being fair". Stacy Lee George

My dad Henry Charles George (Snooks) worked a swing shift at the 3M Company in Decatur, Alabama; he also drove a large truck on his off days traveling to Tennessee delivering clothes for a local sewing factory. Dad seldom had a day off that I can remember but, he involved me in most of his jobs except for the 3M Company. He had a third job driving a bulldozer for a local coalmine company but, I do not remember the coalmine ever giving him a check. He loved driving that dozer though. My life was pretty much normal until age 12 then it changed forever. I will never forget the day our lives changed forever.

I was riding home from basketball practice with my mom. As we started the drive down Saint John Road, I could see what I called simply, "the old house on Julian Road". There were several vehicles there with red lights flashing and one vehicle was an ambulance. You see if my dad had an off day, he was always helping someone usually for free. The ambulance was there to pick up my dad. He was trimming limbs for a neighbor when he fell from a tree only twelve feet. He landed across a top ground root; the tree looked like something out of the fictional tale of the Headless Horseman. The legend of Sleepy Hollow was full of massive trees with large top-ground roots spreading out like the legs of a brown grass spider.

My dad's life changed forever and as for the rest of the family it was as if an EF5 tornado had touched down. There was damage done, but with a lot of work we would all survive. Have you ever noticed when a tornado of this magnitude comes through a community? The trees and buildings come back, but you can always see the scar left behind in the path. My dad was paralyzed from the bottom of his rib cage in his back or near his bellybutton in the front all the way down; he could not even feel a tingle in his toes. The doctors said, "It is not likely he will walk again because bruising of the spinal cord seldom heals." Our new path suddenly became clear, but it would not be easy. Mom decided to stay home taking care of dad and in a few months the disability Social Security check finally arrived. We adjusted our lives to make it all work. I remember the first commodity cheese and powdered milk at the old county barn; that was the best cheese in the world.

The Ryan community and the 3M Corporation raised our family money and we survived until our life was stabilized. Now, this is where my conservative beliefs split from traditional Republicans. I believe in giving people a hand-up but, not a hand-out. I believe most everyone deserves and needs help at some point in their life.

I started working when I was age twelve at Throwers Nursery in Baileyton, Alabama. This was my first real job other than raking leaves for a neighbor. I was too young to use a hoe, so they let me pull those rag weeds by hand. I remember getting that hoe for a brief time. I chopped too many peach trees down and they decided with a good pair of gloves weed pulling was a better method for me. I was excited when I was trained on how to bud and wrap peach trees. This was a two-person team with one budding and one wrapping. I was the youngest of my team, so I was the person who wrapped the bud to the peach tree with a rubber band. My job was to prepare the tree for budding by clearing the leaves from the tree in front of the budding person and stay caught up with the wrapping of the trees. The number that stuck in my head was $16.00/one thousand trees. The budding person got $16.00, and the "wrapper" got sixteen dollars each per one-thousand trees. My last year working there I remember working about 6:30 am to 5:00pm and we were good for about 2500 trees per day at our best. Those days were hot. I will never forget that and all jobs in my life have been easier from that point forward.

Next, I worked construction with Southerland Construction until I graduated from high school. Fred Southerland owned the company, and he was a hardworking businessman. He played a big role in patching our lives back together when my dad was paralyzed. I remember shortly after my dad's accident Fred had a fundraiser at his home. This money helped us until my dad's disability kicked in. I will never forget what the Ryan community done for my family.

I graduated from Brewer High School in June of 1987 on a Friday night, and I started working at Wyle Laboratories in Madison, Alabama on the following Monday morning. Most of my classmates headed to the beach, but I wanted to start making money. I was not jealous of my classmates for going to the beach. I was used to working since I was twelve and I really did not know what a vacation was. My first day at Wyle Laboratories was sweeping trash in the large pit. Over the next ten years I would travel around the United States and build a diverse resume. I worked on the Redstone Arsenal for NASA testing on the Aft Skirt of the Space Shuttle. I worked on projects for the Department of Defense, Boeing, Lockheed Martin, SCI, WPAFB (Wright Patterson Air Force Base), and so on just to name a few. I also worked in nuclear power plants in Arkansas and Louisiana as a VT-3 Inspector. We basically did inspections and testing for the shock absorbers for the pipelines within nuclear power plants. I was stationed for a couple of months in Denver, Colorado putting strain gauges in the fuel tank of the Magellan Space Craft.

The scariest thing happened to me while working at Wyle Laboratories in Madison. I came in from a road trip from Arkansas and several of the guys I returned with were laid off; it was extremely slow back home in Alabama. My boss at the time said, "George you are a good worker, and we want to keep you but, we have a different job we need you to do until things pick up." I was concerned with the pay. My boss said, "we are going to move you to the facility department and leave your pay the same." I was excited and ready to start.

The first few days I went to the office picking up trash and changing light bulbs. The next week my new boss said, "George if you do not mind, we need you to clean some of the toilets." I was fine with that although it was a little awkward at first especially in the women's restrooms. I decided that if I had some large thick rubber gloves and plenty of cleaning supplies this toilet cleaning is not so bad. I quickly noticed that no one else liked cleaning restrooms so I seized the moment. I decided to run it by my supervisor and simply say, "what if I just clean all of the restrooms really good and just touch them up all during the day. This would take me a full 8-hour day.

To shorten this story a bit, I did this job for about six months and during that time I was awarded employee of the month (the only time during my ten years at Wyle Laboratories I achieved this award). Toilet cleaning was going good until our company workload returned. My supervisor stated they needed me back running vibration control in the Dynamics Laboratory. Basically, in Dynamics we would simulate test specimens traveling thousands of miles in seconds on a shaking mechanism. This required me to operate a vibration control computer. I was putting in some long hours doing both jobs until a problem came up. As I was cleaning my bathroom in the main building a normal customer of Wyle Laboratories came in. Later that day, I was asked to report to the Dynamics laboratory to perform a test for the same customer who saw me cleaning a toilet earlier in the day. The customer reported to management that the janitor was now operating the vibration control computer in the lab. That was my last day working for both departments, so I chose to go back to the Dynamics Laboratory, because I could no longer do both jobs. I tell you this story for one reason. Whatever comes my way, by the grace of GOD, I find a way to carry on my mission to survive this game of life that we all live. Also, I was a state certified life insurance agent for Modern Woodmen of America, selling life insurance at night while working at Wyle Laboratories during the day.

In 1997 I was contacted about a better opportunity with a lot more pay, as well as 20 miles closer to home working for the Amtec Corporation. Bud Albritton owned the company, and I learned a lot watching Bud run his company. I worked in the control room running vibration control like my job at Wyle Laboratories. I also worked in the machinery maintenance, and I worked on high voltage amplifiers. While at Wyle Laboratories with just on the job training, I learned about high voltage amplifiers. As a portion of my new job opportunity, I made a commitment to go to school at night. As I began my schooling at Calhoun Community College in the field of electronics I stumbled across a course in Political Science.

I was absolutely fascinated with politics and my instructor Dr. Waymon Burke nominated me for the 1999 Political Science Student of the Year at Calhoun College; I won that award later that year. GOD has a way of lining people up with the gift he gave them in life. Not many of us find the gift GOD gave us because we are too hard-headed. This political event triggered a three-year campaign to eventually be elected as the first Republican County Commissioner in Morgan County during modern printed history or since Reconstruction. My first run was in 2000. Next, I won re-election in 2004 by a large margin. In 2006 I ran for Sheriff between Commission terms, and it cost me my reelection for Commissioner in 2008. The election date for Sheriff was 6/6/06; I should have known with a date like that this race was going to be interesting. Most people say that run for sheriff hurt me at that moment. Several years later that Sheriff went to jail on issues of keeping left over jail food money for personal use that I centered my campaign on years earlier.

In early 2009 GOD put me in prison I tell people. I started working for the Department of Corrections as a cadet. Later that year I would go to Selma, Alabama, and graduate from the Corrections Academy with APOST-c certification to use a 40 caliber Glock and a 12-gauge shotgun. In 2014 I made a run for Governor in the Republican Primary against a popular incumbent GOP Governor at the time. Governor Robert Bentley took a plunge shortly after his reelection and could not likely win dog catcher in Alabama now. During this election we spent less than twenty-five thousand dollars and Governor Bentley spent millions winning the Republican Primary easily, but I did come in a very distant second in a three-man race. For now, my slogan is "Let

Stacy Lee George Do It Alabama". GOD only knows what is next, but I am not done. I hope this book inspires people to get active in politics and this book should point a person in the direction of corruption along with misuse of taxpayer money. It starts in the dark when nobody is looking, and it seldom ends until they are caught.

What causes a twist in ethical thinking? How does such mentality form? It must have a foundation of darkness, where the person in power finds an area (or areas) where there is little knowledge of what is going on by any (or few). This is where the good ole boy, "you scratch my back and I will look the other way", takes place; neither of which stands up to accountability.

Lots of times an ordinary (non-political) average Joe (or Jolene) will spot the discrepancy – Notice the odd, with no means of shedding light. This average Joe can many times be fed a line of contrived legal jargon and go on their daily way. I soon became the middleman in this scenario. I listened, looked, researched and if I saw true corruption taking place, I would act immediately.

At this point I would like to address a viewpoint created mostly by those who felt I disjointed their crooked means of gain. Their only defense was to make it seem my desire for doing the right thing was an oddness, as if this in some way I made the actual wrongness (often criminal) to be right. The problem I faced was when I brought this corruption to the light it was often in the newspaper and sometimes the television. This marked me as a political gadfly.

If anyone has been led to believe this way – please consider the very paragraph you have just read. Would you rather have an employee who took from your business or one who found ways to save you money? These people were your employees- the business - your government.

It is my hope with this writing that more people will notice the odd – follow the money – ask questions and bring things to light. It is also my hope that with the thought of being caught by a more aware public that corruption will be prevented before it occurs. I notice when I am around, politicians seem to be concerned; a little of that is not a bad thing.

Was this a witch-hunt? Why did this have to be made public? The answer is yes and the reason a witch was publicly hung was to put fear in the rest of the witches. The facts were there in these cases unlike a typical witch-hunt and there were no doubt politicians who did not want to be politically hung. These are the true stories of a hunt to find justice.

In the following pages are many of the times that fired up furnace burning inside me was unleashed. The short stories are backed up by actual newspaper articles about the described corruption, misuse of money, and things just done in the dark. Hopefully it will show the many ways these things happen, what to look for, and what to do about them. Cleaning house takes a community, but do not expect to leave with a reward for what you do. You can just get used to the word gadfly. This is not all the misuse of money and corruption I found. These are only a few of the articles and only a fraction of what I witnessed happening.

1 Chronicles 4:10

And Jabez called on the God of Israel saying, "Oh, that You would bless me indeed, and enlarge my territory, that Your hand would be with me, and that You would keep *me* from evil, that I may not cause pain!" So God granted him what he requested.

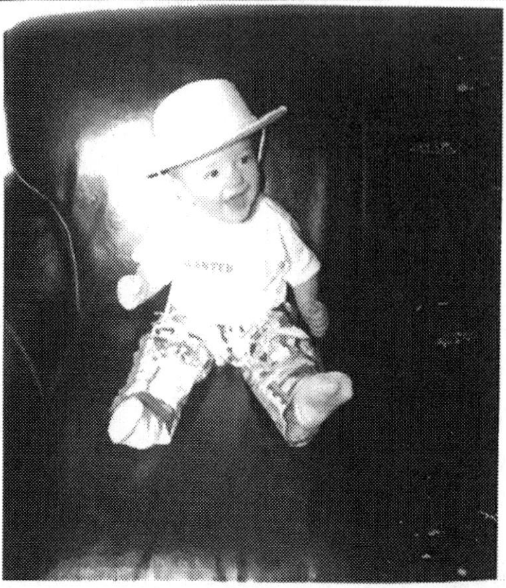

'The biggest mistake I ever made'

Former Commissioner Stacy George says his bid for sheriff was ill advised

By Sheryl Marsh
smarsh@decaturdaily.com
340-2437

Since his defeat in the 2010 Republican primary that ousted him off the Morgan County Commission, Former District 4 Commissioner Stacy George has lived through testing and training.

The result is a badge that he displays as a uniform as a correctional officer at Limestone Correctional Facility.

Although he's not a judge, George, 47, says he has no intention of running for that office this year's election.

George ran for sheriff against incumbent Greg Bartlett in the 2010 GOP primary and had a significant loss.

"Reaching for sheriff is probably the biggest mistake I ever made in my life," said George. "Looking back now after being in law enforcement almost a year. You need several years of law enforcement experience before you run for sheriff."

"I started as a correctional officer," he explained. "Then I went to the law enforcement academy in Selma. It was hard work physically and mentally taxing. The three months I spent in school were good for me because it taught me how to work with people better. You cannot raise prison stress. It takes teamwork."

George said his class started with 108 students but 131 graduated in his weather and he was his full academically.

"This is an accomplishment of which I am very proud," he said. "I am also proud of what I was able to do on the County Corrections."

The school board district voted recently flipped back in the Rock board.

He said he plans to make a decision about running for the seat soon in two weeks.

Former District 4 Morgan County Commissioner Stacy George, is now a correctional officer at Limestone Correctional Facility. He says the job, he said, helps people this live a sheriff should have several years experience in law enforcement.

Daily photo by John McCarey

Stacy George receives recognition at Calhoun

Stacy George of Buckeye has been selected in the Most Outstanding Student in Political Science at Calhoun Community College. He received the award during the college's 15th Annual Awards Day ceremonies recently.

George was inducted into the Sigma Lambda Chapter of Phi Theta Kappa honor society in recognition of his academic achievements. It is his top honor.

He is employed by Aerojet Corporation of Huntsville known in Huntsville as an engineering technician and is currently applying his political science education through an active involvement in local and state politics.

Stacy George was selected Most Outstanding Student in Political Science at Calhoun Community College at the 15th Annual Awards Day ceremony.

elle
ck?

FRONT B1

COLLEGE SCOREBOARD

Mississippi State	29	Florida	41	So. Mississippi	33
Alabama	7	South Carolina	21	UAB (2OT)	30
Tennessee	63	Auburn	29	Alabama A&M	27
Arkansas	20	Georgia (OT)	26	Alcorn State	20
Vanderbilt	24	LSU	20	UNA	21
Kentucky	20	Ole Miss	9	West Alabama	14

Gala XVI honorees

LIVING

THE DECATUR DAILY

SUNDAY, NOVEMBER 12, 2000

Morgan's 1st GOP commissioner

Stacy George worked entire county looking for new supporters

By Sheryl Marsh

Both sides of town

Please see George, page A8

Stacy George will be sworn in as Morgan County's newest commissioner Monday.

George

Continued from page A1

Who is Stacy George?

Commission goals

Dad

THE DECATUR DAILY

Wednesday, June 2, 2004

George collects most votes in Morgan

He defeats 2 others in District 4 contest

By Sheryl Marsh
Staff writer

Morgan County District 4 Commissioner Stacy George overcame opposition from members of his party, not from the GOP nomination, and received more votes than any of the other two candidates in Tuesday's primary election.

George, 36, garnered 52.3 percent of the vote over Tom Kennemer, 28 percent and Terry Brown's 187 percent, according to unofficial vote totals. He received 4,275 votes to become the county's top local vote-getter and was not challenged in November's general election.

"Going one on one with the people made the difference, I think," George said. "We went all over the county including Northwest Decatur. I didn't wave out anybody. My job is to work for all the people in the county."

Please see George, page A8

George

Continued from page A1

not put a select few, and that's the message I wanted to relay to the people of our grand community."

Despite a letter that a member of the Morgan County Republican Party circulated to rural appositions against him, George emerged a winner throughout the county, including his boxes in Decatur.

During the campaign he also became embroiled in a battle with fellow Republican Amanda Scott, the county's revenue commissioner. George questioned hundreds of phone calls charged to taxpayers between Scott and a revenue commissioner in another county. He also questioned why she didn't return in a timely manner an unemployment check that the county advanced her for travel to a meeting.

Then Scott questioned long-distance telephone calls from George's district when her husband, David Scott, an official with the state Republican Party, became Kennemer's campaign manager.

top campaign contributor in the last round of financial disclosures.

"I motioned to work hard and I took a higher road than those who were against me," George said.

Remember, 42, said he is disappointed, but wishes George well.

"I wanted to be the next commissioner but the voters have made their decision and I respect that. I offer my congratulations to Stacy George, the winner. It was an experience and I had a lot of fun and met some wonderful people. I'll cherish that for a long time," said Kennemer, a former TV news anchor.

Attempts to reach Brown were unsuccessful. Brown was the top spender in the race, loaning thousands to his own campaign.

Completing his first term, George became the first Republican commissioner in 2000 when he defeated former Commissioner Howard Jenkins, who had served 12 years.

George will face Rickey Borden, the Democratic nominee, in the November general election.

My friend Cousin Darryl

DECATUR DAILY

Wednesday, February 1, 2006

Morgan County Commissioner Stacy George announced Tuesday this week plans to run for sheriff.

George files for sheriff

HOW DID AN OUTSIDER LIKE STACY LEE GEORGE WIN?

I decided to put this chapter in after much thought and prayer. I have concluded I can best serve the cause for fighting corruption by telling you what I know. I want to imagine thousands of people with some of the knowledge I have gained over a twenty-five-year period. What good is accomplished to only explain how to find corruption, if I do not explain how to get a common man or woman elected? The first hint is they cannot see you coming because if you get on the radar the corrupt folks will try to stop you. I would suggest you take one course in political science at your local Junior College. Politics is a science, and you need to understand basic government functions. You need to have a backbone, or this is a waste of time. Do not imagine yourself on this white horse riding into town and getting the bad guys then riding into the sunset. Think of the worst 10 things you have ever done. Imagine 7 of them will likely come out when you enter politics. The 7 that come out are not in any certain order. This is not meant to scare you, but simply to make you think before entering. It depends somewhat on the office you are seeking. Someone seeking a city council position would not be put to the test as much as someone seeking state senate. If you are under 18 going into politics, I would suggest you be cautious who you hang out with. I would also suggest you stay single as long as possible because once you marry you take on the personal baggage of two people. Every person has baggage, but some have more than others. GOD created only one perfect and that was Jesus Christ.

I become interested in politics after taking a course in political science in the late 1990's. I tried many things to increase my name identification, and these are some of the ways I did just that. Keep in mind social media was almost non-existent at the time. I am giving you information that will allow someone with little or very little money to run a competitive local race. This is based on a population of just over sixty-thousand registered voters.

I started by simply leaving cards that said Stacy George-Republican Morgan County with a phone number. I put an address and two elephants on the cards. I left these in country stores all over Morgan County. I would not leave too many because people will throw them away; always leave ten or less. This next part is very important, and nobody really does this. I would take off work on special elections within the county. Municipal elections are going on as well. You can stand the legal distance from the polling station; I think the distance is still 30 feet from the door. I simply just gave people a card and said, "I am not on your ballot". I just simply wanted to meet voters. I started this process two years before I made my run. This process is tricky because you do not want to be pushy just available. This process is effective, and you are just meeting the people who really vote. All you need is a dove bucket or a lawn chair. You need a few packs of peanut butter crackers and plenty of liquids if it is hot. You might get some negative feedback, but overall, this process is effective.

There is another important secret. I had no opposition in the Republican Primary that year, so I paid around one-hundred and fifty dollars to run as a delegate to the Republican National Convention. I ran against sitting Alabama Attorney General Bill Pryor and now he is an appointed Federal Judge. Of course, Pryor beat me; losing was my plan. I could not afford to go to the convention, and I picked Place 4 because I was running for Morgan County Commission District #4. You see people do not pay close attention to these delegate races. My thinking was for one-hundred and fifty bucks I could be on every ballot in Alabama during the Republican Primary. I lost the delegate run, but I appeared on the ballot later that November. I think the qualifying fee to run for county commission was 250 dollars since we had no Republicans elected to the county commission at the time. I knew that in the November election people could do a split ticket vote. This means you can vote straight Democrat or Republican. This also means you can mark straight Democrat or Republican at the top of the ballot and still mark an individual Republican down the ballot if you want to. This is an important secret people look over easily or people simply do not know. I will repeat a second time. A person can mark the straight ticket then down the ballot you can mark a candidate on the other side in a different party. This is important, so I will say it another way a third time. You can mark straight Democrat and vote for Republican Stacy Lee George down the ballot and Stacy Lee George will get a vote along with all other Democrat candidates except the one Republican you marked.

I studied the ADC (Alabama Democrat Caucus) and I watched these folks give out this yellow ballot. These ballots are given out primarily in the black community voting precincts. I made a yellow sample ballot that was very similar to the ADC sample ballot and my sample ballot marked straight Democrat at the top of the ballot marking Stacy Lee George on the Republican side. This allowed me to get a vote as a Republican. I gave out 500 sample ballots yellow in color that November, and I was 30 feet from the entrance to the largest polling place in the black community. After about 10 hours I ran out of sheets and a lady was nice enough to bring me some of the sheets left behind after people voted. I redistributed around 25 of those until I ran out again then headed to the house. I won my election by less than one hundred votes, and I received approximately 150 votes at that polling place. Now, this will not work in a Democrat or Republican primary vote. I have tried this without success, so you are wasting your time unless something changes in the voting process. This is only effective in a general election process. These tactics are very important to know. This only works if people in a community know who you are. I spent over 2 years just meeting people door to door. I never really spoke to a group. I never introduced my family or anything.

How many signs did I use? Not many and I think I had two large signs. The two I had made were of banner material and I moved them once per week before work. I put over two-hundred thousand miles on my vehicle in a little over 2 years' time. This did include a 60-mile round trip drive to work from eastern Morgan County to south Huntsville. My father did scrape up enough money to get me about 50 small signs a few weeks before the election. We already had the wires because after elections were over whoever did not get their signs up, I did my duty helping clean up the roads. I would ask candidates if they wanted their signs and if so, I would return them. Most candidates did not want them back allowing me to collect a fair number of wires for small signs. Over 25 years I have accumulated many scrap wires even some old signs. Those larger signs are usually printed on one side. I reused a lot of those signs and I always used vinyl letters instead of screen-printing large signs. You can just peel off the letters and put more on when using vinyl. I used about 20 signs in the 2014 Governor race that I reused for a ten-year period. I put them all out in the Mobile and Baldwin County area because I could not afford to travel there very much.

Did I really go to Point Mallard Water Park in Decatur, Alabama and ask them to page for Stacy George during the busy season to build name identification? Yes, I did, but I cannot recommend this as a campaign tool. I normally wore flip flops because I love those things. I would wear a golf shirt and some khaki shorts. I love those tank tops, but people let me know that was not good to wear; I reluctantly listened. What I did not listen to is of most importance. People would continuously tell me I did not have a chance. If you are on the ballot, you always have a chance. The odds may not be good, but you do have a chance. The fact that George Bush Jr. for President was on the top of the ballot that November helped me as well. During a Presidential election in Alabama local Republican candidates have always done well. If you pay attention some County Commission races run with the president while others run with the Governor race. These are called staggered elections. I knew this as well and if you pay attention, you will know also.

The year is now 2021 and I have taken my time writing this book. It was started in I believe 2013 if my memory serves me correct. I pondered and procrastinated, but I never gave up. I do not know what the future may hold, but GOD knows. GOD put this adventure in my heart, and I could say," I wish I had done some things different". I will not say that because during this adventure I had some wonderful children and I met Karen Brewster George. Karen is my best friend and my beautiful wife. She is my soul mate and if you have never met your soul mate you are not really living your life to the fullest. I pray you find that person. I also pray it takes you less time and less failed relationships including many marriages to complete this task.

This book proves what one man can do with GOD'S favor over a twenty-five-year span of cleaning up corruption from the Morgan County Courthouse to the Governor's House in Montgomery, Alabama. One man with people feeding him clues along the way and some tenacious reporting by the news media can do so much. You see I started in politics to find good honest people to run for political office. My goal has never changed and these writings in this book will serve as a roadmap to minimize corruption in Alabama while inspiring a new group of less corrupt politicians. Stay tuned because," I am not done".

James 4:10 ESV

Humble yourselves in the sight of the Lord, and He will lift you up.

Proverbs 3:34 ESV

Toward the scorners he is scornful, but to the humble he gives favor.

VOTE &
RE-ELECT
STACY LEE
GEORGE
MORGAN CO.
COMMISSIONER,
DISTRICT 4

Pol Ad Paid for by the Friends
to Re-Elect Stacy George

Elect the 1st. Republican to the Morgan County Commission

Stacy George
Commission District #4 (November)
election at-large not by district...
Approximately 70,000 voters in Morgan County

Also June 6th. Primary
Stacy George (Bush) delegate place 4
Entire state of Alabama...

We need to send someone from North Alabama to
Philadelphia...

JUST LEAVE IT TO GEORGE !

GEORGE BUSH JR.
AND
STACY GEORGE

From the Courthouse to the White house

Stacy
Lee
GEORGE
Morgan
County
Commission

District 4

November 7th
Republican?

Pol. Ad. by Stacy George
PO Box 202, Somerville, AL

Banner Signs

Banner Signs

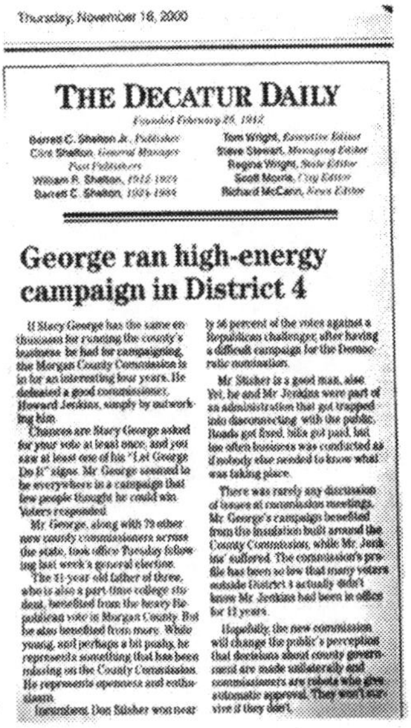

Thursday, November 16, 2000

THE DECATUR DAILY
Founded February 26, 1912

Barrett C. Shelton Jr. *Publisher*   Tom Wright, *Executive Editor*
Clint Shelton *General Manager*   Steve Stewart, *Managing Editor*
Past Publishers   Regina Wright, *State Editor*
William R. Shelton, 1912-1929   Scott Morris, *City Editor*
Barrett C. Shelton, 1929-1989   Richard McCann, *News Editor*

George ran high-energy campaign in District 4

If Stacy George has the same enthusiasm for running the county's business he had for campaigning, the Morgan County Commission is in for an interesting four years. He defeated a good commissioner, Howard Jenkins, simply by out-working him.

Chances are Stacy George asked for your vote at least once, and you saw at least one of his "Let George Do It" signs. Mr. George seemed to be everywhere in a campaign that few people thought he could win. Voters responded.

Mr. George, along with 79 other new county commissioners across the state, took office Tuesday following last week's general election.

The 41-year-old father of three, who is also a part-time college student, benefited from the heavy Republican vote in Morgan County. But he also benefited from more. While young, and perhaps a bit pushy, he represents something that has been missing on the County Commission. He represents openness and enthusiasm.

Incumbent Don Slisher won near-

ly 56 percent of the votes against a Republican challenger after having a difficult campaign for the Democratic nomination.

Mr. Slisher is a good man, also. Yet, he and Mr. Jenkins were part of an administration that got trapped into disconnecting with the public. Roads got fixed, bills got paid, but too often business was conducted as if nobody else needed to know what was taking place.

There was rarely any discussion of issues at commission meetings. Mr. George's campaign benefited from the insulation built around the County Commission, while Mr. Jenkins' suffered. The commission's profile has been so low that many voters outside District 4 actually didn't know Mr. Jenkins had been in office for 12 years.

Hopefully the new commission will change the public's perception that decisions about county government are made unilaterally and commissioners are robots who give automatic approval. They won't survive if they don't.

Let *Stacy Lee* Do It
GEORGE
Morgan Co.
Commission
District #4

We Need a Conservative Voice in the Commission
The Back Side Explains Why

Pol Co. By Friends To Stacy George PO Box 202, Somerville, AL

The Arab Tribune

'The Ledger of Community Progress'

George running for Morgan commission

George

A STAFF REPORT
The Arab Tribune

Stacy Lee George says it's payback time.

When he was 13, his father was trimming a neighbor's tree, fell and paralyzed himself. The people in Ryan and surrounding communities held fundraisers to help out the family until Social Security kicked in. Also, his father's employer, 3M in Decatur, was good to his dad.

That's part of the reason he's running for the Republican nomination for Morgan County Commission District 4.

George said he wants the opportunity to give back something to the people of Morgan County, who have given so much to him and his family.

In the June 6 primary, he is also running

■ Please see GEORGE, Page 3A

George

■ Continued from Page 1A

as a state delegate to the Republican convention in Philadelphia. He more than jokingly said he likes the ring of George Bush Jr. and Stacy Lee George.

George said he's been locally active in Republican races and in the last two years has registered numerous voters in Morgan County.

He has also been actively pushing for legislation to change voting in Morgan County from an at-large system in which all 70,000 voters elect all four commissioners, to district voting.

He said that last year he collected 1,000 petition names to help get a local bill passed for a referendum on district voting in Morgan County and, if that fails, he plans to push for a statewide bill.

Of the state's 67 counties, only 14 have at-large elections. In Morgan's case, half of the county's registered voters live in Decatur and another 13 percent live in Hartselle. Only 37 percent of the voters live in Districts 3 and 4.

That's why it's not surprising, George said, that since changing to at-large elections in 1971, every candidate who has carried District 4 has been defeated by the "Decatur" vote. The local choice, he said, has been defeated, and that's not right.

"I feel I could offer Morgan County a voice that would represent the rural areas as well as represent a pro-business outlook in the urban areas of Morgan County," George said.

And if that takes work, he indicated he can handle that. He said he's been working since he was 12, starting at Thomas's Nursery at Baileyton. He worked summer jobs for Southerland Construction until he graduated from Brewer High School in 1987.

Three days later, he said, he started to work doing testing for Wyle Laboratories in Huntsville. In 1997 he took a better job with Amtec Corp. doing electronic maintenance on high voltage amplifiers and hydraulic installations on the Redstone Arsenal. In 1999, Amtec promoted him to a engineering technician support contractor on the arsenal, a position he still holds.

Also in 1997, George started school year-round at Calhoun College of North Alabama. Last year, he was named Political Science Student of the Year and made a member of Phi Theta Kappa honor society. He is also on the Board of Political Archivers at Calhoun and made the 1999 National Honor Society.

"I plan many years of future college courses to better my education," George said. "I (now) take only one course a quarter not to interfere with my religious, family and work duties."

Staff Photo by Dan Henry
Stacy George, a Republican candidate for Morgan County Commission, listens to a question.

Tuesday, June 3rd Let George Do It...

THE DECATUR DAILY

Election

WEDNESDAY, NOVEMBER 8, 2000

Morgan Co. Commission

100% of precincts in county

DISTRICT 3		
■ Don Stisher (D)	[illegible]	[illegible]
☐ Wayne Propps (R)	[illegible]	[illegible]
DISTRICT 4		
☐ Howard Jenkins (D)	[illegible]	[illegible]
■ Stacy L. George (R)	[illegible]	[illegible]

Unofficial Morgan County precinct-by-precinct results from Tuesday's elections

Race / Candidate	Precinct results	Countywide total
President of the United States		
Al Gore (D)	[illegible]	[illegible]
Harry Browne (L)	[illegible]	[illegible]
G.W. Bush (R)	[illegible]	[illegible]
Pat Buchanan (I)	[illegible]	[illegible]
John Hagelin (I)	[illegible]	[illegible]
Ralph Nader (I)	[illegible]	[illegible]
Howard Phillips (I)	[illegible]	[illegible]
Chief justice of the Alabama Supreme Court		
Sharon Yates (D)	[illegible]	[illegible]
Roy Moore (R)	[illegible]	[illegible]
Morgan County Commission, District 3		
Don Stisher (D)	[illegible]	[illegible]
Wayne Propps (R)	[illegible]	[illegible]
Morgan County Commission, District 4		
Howard Jenkins (D)	[illegible]	[illegible]
Stacy Lee George (R)	[illegible]	[illegible]
Morgan County Board of Education, District 1		
Billy J. Rhodes (D)	[illegible]	[illegible]
Write-in votes	[illegible]	[illegible]
Morgan County Board of Education, District 5		
Kenneth Joe Razor (D)	[illegible]	[illegible]
Jimmy A. Dobbs (R)	[illegible]	[illegible]
Edwin Sutton (I)	[illegible]	[illegible]
Amendment 1 (trust funds)		
Yes	[illegible]	[illegible]
No	[illegible]	[illegible]
Amendment 2 (interracial marriage)		
Yes	[illegible]	[illegible]
No	[illegible]	[illegible]
Amendment 5 (Auburn University trustees)		
Yes	[illegible]	[illegible]
No	[illegible]	[illegible]

Courtesy of the Decatur Daily / writer Sheryl Marsh

Best friend and Soul mate

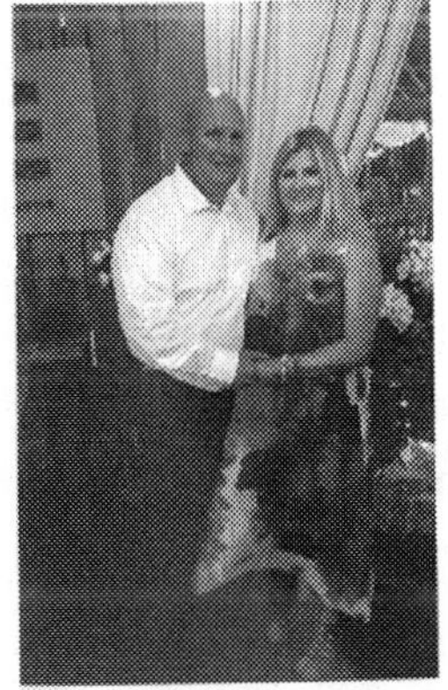

Country Boy Eddy Event

Holiday Inn Decatur AL
Event

I won!

Stacy George takes a congratulatory phone call from his opponent Howard Jenkins Tuesday evening at his home after George found out he won Dist. 4.

Photo by Corey Wilson 11-7-00

Country Boy Eddy

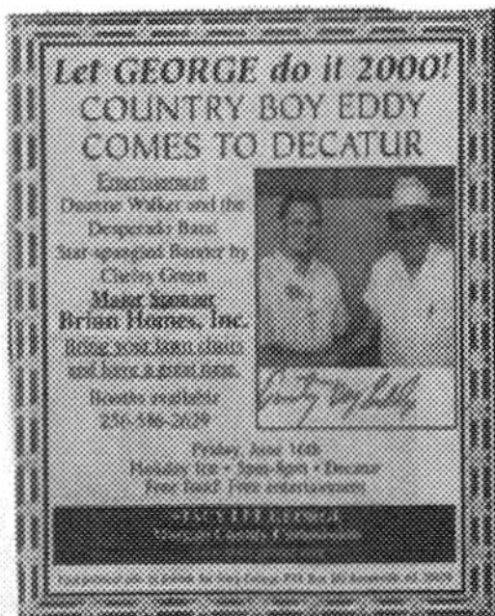
Let GEORGE do it 2000!
COUNTRY BOY EDDY
COMES TO DECATUR
Brian Homes, Inc.

Let Stacy Lee Do It!
GEORGE
Morgan County Commission
District 4
• Bring diversity to the commission.
• We need a conservative voice!
Experience and Education

CORRUPTION ALWAYS HAS A FACE

Corruption can be written into words through basic specifications of a bid process or in a piece of legislation. Over the past twenty-five years I have monitored politics and witnessed variations of what I consider bid rigging multiple times. I have also seen creative ways to get around the bidding process. There is a need for certain specifications to meet the basic need of the product or equipment. Watch for local bids that come in with only one bidder. What happens is the politician receives money from a certain equipment provider. The bid specifications will be an almost mirror to the actual specifications of the product/ equipment who gives the politician money. The other bidders that have comparable products simply remain silent because they did not meet the specifications. This is how the buddy system works. This is hard to trace sometimes because cash is given, or they simply donate to politicians through a Political Action Committee (PAC) to disguise the contribution. Also, corruption creeps in through professional services. Politicians use this with architect firms and attorney services a lot. Have you ever noticed the same attorney firm stays in place throughout decades of politicians? Have you ever noticed an expensive piece of equipment being used throughout the entire county even though you know there are cheaper equipment dealers with a good product out there? Occasionally, you will see these politicians throw a bone out there for the other product/equipment buyers to get. This simply keeps the other vendors with some hope and keeps the talk to a minimum.

How do we stop this? You try to elect people who are not necessarily in the click on a local level. All you need is one politician on a city council, county commission, school board, electric board, water board, etc. This is not an impossible task on a local level. This is harder to do in a state legislative level, but not impossible. On a statewide level it is almost impossible. This is the reason these state house seats, and state senate seats are so important. Now, on a United States House seat or United States Senate seat it is almost impossible as well. We must rely on the Alabama Ethics Commission to keep the politicians on a local level and state level in check. We must press politicians to fund more positions and more funding for the Alabama Ethics Commission. There should be a constant presence of the Alabama Ethics Commission in every county in the state. The only hope taxpayers have is the fact someone is holding the politicians accountable. Corruption does always have a face. If you look deep enough in the wording of specifications and trace who benefits from these specifications to a person you will find the corruption in the Heart of Dixie.

2 Peter 2:19 TPT

They promise others freedom, yet they themselves are slaves to corruption, for people are slaves to whatever overcomes them.

Psalm 119:36

Incline my heart to Your testimonies
And not to dishonest gain.

Morgan picks Tennessee jail designer; George balks

Stacy George

By Sheryl Marsh

Three Morgan County commissioners voted Monday to select a Tennessee architectural firm to sketch the county's new jail.

On a recommendation from District 3 Commissioner Don Stisher, Commissioners Jeff Clark and Faye Sparkman voted with him to choose Hart, Freeland and Roberts Inc. of Brentwood, Tenn. District 4 Commissioner Stacy George abstained from voting, saying the commissioners rushed the deal.

▶ Synopsis, C2

The commission chose the firm over four Alabama companies, including Pearson, Humphries and Jones Architects Inc., which designed many of the facilities at Calhoun Community College. Stisher said, however, the chosen firm will agree to allow School Design Group of Decatur to assist with the design plan. School can offer input about the design to make it compatible with other downtown facilities because of its experience here, George said.

Stisher said the Tennessee firm was highly recommended.

George, who asked School to make a presentation with the other companies last month, said he thought the commission should wait because the general election is near. He said the rushed selection is politically motivated because Chairman Larry Bennich might lose voting power on the commission if GOP candidates replace Sparkman and Clark in the general election.

"I am for School, but I think one of the other companies would have allowed [illegible]

Please see Jail, page C2

Larry Bennich

Jail

Continued from page C1

them to work on the project with them, especially since they're Alabama-based. On the other hand, I abstained from voting because I believe the commission's action is political since it's so close to the election," George said after the meeting.

"I feel like the chairman has made up his mind what he wants to do and if he does not go forward, he may not have the votes to pass his agenda for the handpick of the group he wants to design the jail, if the people elect two new commissioners."

Bennich did not make the recommendation, and said he did not show favoritism.

"I'm sorry he (George) feels that way because that was a total decision of the board. I recommended all those people who came in and presented proposals, they're all well qualified," Bennich said.

He told the commissioners Monday that they needed to decide on an architect because of a 2008 deadline that a federal judge gave the county to build a jail. The judge made the order based on a consent decree and attorneys a year ago.

Although the county has three years to build a jail, Bennich said it will take time to get to the point of construction, which will also require a lot of time.

None of the firms that presented proposals gave estimated costs for the jail, which will have about 400 beds. The location will be on First Avenue Northeast on a lot the county owns near the Morgan County Area Transportation Service building.

Stisher made the recommendation and Bennich called for individual votes. When George abstained, Stisher questioned it.

He told George that everybody needed to vote in agreement on the issue and he asked if his abstention was a "no" vote.

County Attorney Bill Shinn explained to Stisher that George's abstention was not a vote and that he and any of the other commissioners have the right to abstain from voting on an issue.

Clark said he voted for Hart, Freeland and Roberts because the company impressed him with its experience in designing correctional facilities and because it emphasized designing a jail with staffing in mind.

Sparkman said she voted for the firm because it would get input from School.

George said during negotiations that he wants the Tennessee company to include School's participation in a contract. The commission authorized Bennich to negotiate with Hart, Freeland and Roberts.

In addition to PH&J, other architectural firms that made presentations to the commission were HKW Inc. of Birmingham; Goodwyn, Mills and Cawood Inc. of Birmingham; and 2WR of Montgomery.

THE DECATUR DAILY

ERFR[illegible]

Tuesday, August 24, 2004

Politicking charged in Morgan jail caulk bids

By Sheryl Marsh

Morgan County commissioners accused each other of politicking Monday when they argued over accepting a bid from a Tennessee company to caulk the new jail.

Jim Davis, construction manager, presented bids that he received for caulking the jail, a job he said would take place a year from now.

He recommended that the commission approve the low bid from JWC Specialties, a Nashville company. This sparked the ire of District 4 Commissioner Stacy George, who objected to giving a general trades project contract to Nashville-based Hardaway Construction Co. last month.

Stacy George

George noted that a caulking bid from ABG, which has a Birmingham office in addition to one in Tennessee, was $137,150 and one from JWC was $49,000.

"This is a big difference in those bids," George said. "Did the company in state bid on the same specifications as the one in Tennessee?"

Davis said both companies had the same specifications.

George then asked him to call ABG to make sure the specifications were the same as those on which JWC bid.

Davis said he would do so during a break after the work session.

George asked if he could participate in the conversation and Davis said no.

During the commission meeting that followed the work session, Chairman Larry Bennich asked for a motion to approve the low bid and District 1 Commissioner Jeff Clark made the motion, saying that it is a good bid.

George asked to table the matter until the next meeting to make sure the companies were bidding on the same items because Davis said he did not reach ABG during the recess.

District 3 Commissioner Don Stisher, who seconded Clark's motion, said the commission should approve the

Please see Bids, page C2

E DECATUR DAILY

Tuesday, August 3, 2004

Morgan discusses jail money in private

Bennich says meetings with financial adviser didn't violate law

By Sheryl Marsh

Rather than meeting in public, Morgan County commissioners met individually Monday with a financial adviser and Chairman Larry Bennich to discuss borrowing an additional $13 million for a jail.

This would bring the total borrowed to $31 million.

Commissioners John Glasscock, Stacy George and Jeff Clark met one at a time with Johnny Deal of Joe Jolly and Co. Inc. and Bennich.

Dennis Bailey, general counsel for the Alabama Press Association, said officials hold such meetings to get around the open meetings law.

"What they're doing is obviously trying to circumvent the open meetings law by meeting in small groups less than a quorum to keep the public out of the full process," Bailey said. "It's an example of why our public meetings law needs to be changed to include meetings of this type. You would think they would hold an open meeting to discuss money of that amount, but apparently they're afraid to do that for some reason."

Bennich said he didn't intend to skirt the sunshine law.

"In the past, they had been talking about they didn't have time to study anything," he said of commissioners, "so we had Johnny Deal come over and told them if they wanted to come in and talk to him they could."

Although he called special meetings last month concerning jail bids, Bennich said he had the single meetings so that Deal could educate each commissioner about obtaining the bond issues.

Please see Jail, page A8

Jail

Continued from page A1

Clark said there was no need for a special meeting.

"We did not make any decisions in there because we did not have a quorum. I got information concerning the financial situation and Mr. Deal explained details of the options we have," Clark said.

"This was an effort to arm everybody with information they needed to make a good decision," Clark said. "In the past, there's been claims that some commissioners that information was being withheld, and this was to give everybody the information at the same time. It allows us a week to digest the information and ask questions if we feel we need to."

The commission borrowed $18 million last year to build the jail, and Glasscock and George questioned the urgency to borrow additional money. Glasscock said he was pleased with the answer he received that interest rates could increase.

"Mr. Deal estimated that a rise of one point would equate to about $2 million more that we would have to pay back," said Glasscock. "It appears that borrowing money will be the best way to go. I've got a lot of information to study between now and the meeting Monday."

Glasscock said he met with Deal, not Bennich, because Bennich was in and out of the room.

"To me it was like talking to a salesperson or looking through a catalog because I wasn't involved in the first bond issues for the jail," said Glasscock. "No decisions were made and no one asked me for a commitment. It was nothing that couldn't have been done in a public meeting, and I don't feel like it was an attempt to hide anything either. I didn't think I was doing anything wrong just by getting information about bonds."

While George briefly attended a session, he said commissioners should have met in public.

"I questioned why we're in such a hurry because we already have the $18 million we borrowed for the jail," George said. "Also, I want other banks in the county to bid on this, not just give the business to one bank. I'm still not sure this will be the total cost of the jail either since it has gone from $16 million to $18 million and now to 31.

"I told them that it was something that should have been done in a public meeting. And, once I saw what was going on, I left after about 18 minutes. I told them they would know my firm answer when I vote Monday. I never have taken part in secret business and never will."

District 3 Commissioner Don Stisher talked with Deal by phone last week, according to County Administrator Willa Dockery.

In 2001, Montgomery-based 2WR did a feasibility study for a new jail and estimated that it would cost $30 million. Bennich said that was for a 200-bed facility and the new jail will house 400 beds.

Bennich said the group will discuss the issue at a work session Monday before the regular meeting.

"They voted to build a jail, so it's my job to get the money up," Bennich said. "So, I set up a meeting with Mr. Deal to answer their questions. The good thing is that we're not having to raise taxes to build the jail."

Decatur Daily

Thursday, April 24, 2008

Commissioners' practice of hiding behind attorney proving expensive

Morgan County Commission gadfly Stacy George is at it again. Darned him, he's always rocking the courthouse's financial boat.

This week he went after legal fees to the ubiquitous county attorney Bill Shinn. He thinks the county asks for too much legal advice.

He's not questioning the quality of service or the rate per hour that Mr. Shinn charges. He thinks county commissioners should be making more decisions without getting approval from the attorney.

The matter came up this week over Mr. Shinn's March bill for $7,250. The bills, he said, average between $6,000 and $7,000 per month. That's about $75,000 per year.

"It looks like the county is calling on him too much," Commissioner George said.

Indeed, Chairman John Glasscock doesn't venture far into decision-making without consulting Mr. Shinn. Each time he does, that presumably costs taxpayers.

Being cautious is an admirable trait for public officials in today's litigious society.

Sometimes, however, making decisions only involves common sense and fair play, but does require public officials to acquire a degree of expertise in their jobs. Deferring to the county attorney so often suggests commission members don't trust their own decisions.

The practice of consulting the attorney so often has a political side. It provides expensive cover for the commission. If things go wrong, or they pass an unpopular measure, our elected officials can always decline to take responsibility and say "Look, we took our attorney's advice."

Bids

Continued from page C1

bid since it was the lower offer and in accordance with state law.

Playing politics

"All I'm asking for is two weeks, guys, since the amounts are so different. It's no big deal," said George. "But that's all right, the same thing is happening again with a Tennessee company and the same people are pushing it. Something is not right and I would suggest that somebody look into it at a federal level."

"Apparently you are accusing somebody of something," said Bennich.

"We have charged Dooley (Davis' employer) with taking care of bids," Clark said, "and to drag it out like this is political."

"Y'all have made it political," George said. "It's obvious that this commission wants to pass it to hurry up and wait. It's at least a year away before caulking is needed. Who's going to get something out of the deal?"

"I know you're in charge of the meeting, Mr. Chairman, but I'm tired of him accusing us of doing wrong," Stisher told Bennich. "I think you should make him take back what he said. Personally I'm not going to continue to accept it. It's out of order."

"I agree with you that it's out of order," said Bennich.

"Well, I'm not taking nothing back," George said. "I don't see four years so I guess you can keep on doing it."

George cast the lone vote against accepting the caulking bid. District 2 Commissioner John Glasscock did not vote, so Clark and Stisher's votes approved the bid.

Glasscock said after the meeting that he didn't vote because he was still trying to make a decision when Bennich called for the vote.

George and Stisher are running for re-election in November, and Clark and Glasscock are competing against each other for the chairman's post. Republicans George and Glasscock frequently take opposite sides of the positions of Democrats Clark, Stisher and Bennich.

After the meeting Davis said the commission has approved all the jail bids except landscap[illegible]

JESUS CHRIST
IS THE ANSWER
Jesus Christ is the Answer

Bids double jail's cost: $20 million

By Sheryl Marsh

Morgan County commissioners locked in a power struggle today while discussing bids for a new jail that came in twice as high as projected two years ago.

The commission met with the architects who designed the jail and the construction manager to review bids received from companies for 13 projects involved in the construction. The total came in at $20.07 million.

Jim Davis of [illegible] Construction Co., manager of the jail construction, and Steve Griffin of Barr, Freeman and Roberts architectural firm told the commission they would negotiate with the low bidders to reduce the cost.

"Steve and I will work hard to get the price down," Davis said.

Davis presented a detailed report that showed bids for the various categories, and recommended that the commission reject some bids and re-advertise and rebid, and to take under advisement some that might be negotiable.

John Glasscock

Also, commissioners and Sheriff Greg Bartlett agreed they could save nearly $300,000 by having a total brick exterior rather than adding synthetic stone around the building. The county will save an additional $[illegible] by deleting precast cells from the project.

District 4 Commissioner Stacy George and District 3 Commissioner John Glasscock commented on the fact that the cost doubled from the first estimation and expressed concern how they would finance the entire cost.

Larry Bennich

Commission Chairman Larry Bennich and District 1 Commissioner Don Stisher said George and Glasscock should have known a [illegible] facility would cost more than $15 million.

"You can add better than that on your fingers, can't you?" Stisher asked George.

"Y'all ain't bought many cows," Bennich added.

"I've never bought one cow," George said.

A Montgomery firm, 2WR, gave the estimation after doing a feasibility study in 2001 for the jail, which representatives of the company predicted would house 2[illegible]4 inmates.

George suggested that the money should come from the county reserve fund, which Glasscock said has about $[illegible] million.

Bennich said the commission should go back to the bond agent, Joe Jolly Co., which has been the county's financial advisor for years.

Bedford's company?

"Isn't that the same company that Roger Bedford owns, is that not right, Larry?" George asked, referring to the state legislator who's frequently under fire for spending.

"I don't know, but that is the company we've always used," Bennich said.

More than a year ago, the commission borrowed $10 million from the bond company for the jail.

"We should have borrowed more money in the first place," Glasscock said.

Please see Jail, page A8

THE DECATUR DAILY
ERFR(
Tuesday, June 15, 2004

Jail

Continued from page A1

"We did what we should've done at the time we did it," Bennich said.

Power play

George and Glasscock said the final approval for the jail costs should come back to the entire commission for a vote. So the commission unanimously passed a motion for Davis and Bennich to work on the negotiations with bidders, but bring the final costs before the commission for approval.

Near the end of the meeting, however, Stisher moved that Bennich have the power to approve final costs.

"Mr. Stisher, I think that should come back before this commission and we should have the final say," Glasscock said.

"I don't know what the big deal is," said George. "It's not that we don't trust Larry, but the whole commission should give the final approval."

Bennich took a vote on Stisher's motion, on which he and District 1 Commissioner Jeff Clark voted yes and Glasscock and George voted no. Bennich broke the tie and voted with Clark and Stisher to give himself final authority.

ECATUI
Wednesday, March 17, 2004

GOP vs. George: Ouster plotted?

Letter circulated here solicits Republican election opponent

By Sheryl Marsh

A letter that a member of the Morgan County Republican Party circulated in October advertised District 4 Commissioner Stacy George's job and offered fund-raising help for candidates who would accept the offer.

It's not unusual for the party to seek candidates for vacant offices or those held by Democrats, but George is a Republican.

Stacy George
District 4 Morgan commissioner

Bill Wood, the GOP member who sent the letter, acknowledged that three or four others made up a steering committee to select candidates, but he refused to give their names.

"That's a group of people that don't want their names given out," said Wood.

George, who is completing his first term, said he takes it personally and has his thoughts about who the unnamed Republicans are who seek to get him out of office.

"I consider it to be a personal attack and obviously I don't blame the people who make up the whole party and are not participating in these efforts," George said. "A chosen few have made the decision to come out against me. I believe the others Mr. Wood refers to include someone who had their own political agenda."

George wouldn't say who he thought the other members were.

Please see George, page A8

Glasscock's vote keeps Bill Shinn as Morgan's county attorney

By Sheryl Marsh

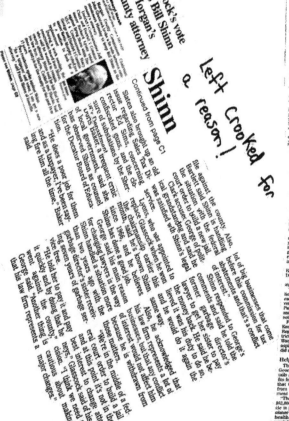

[illegible]

Shinn

Continued from page C1

Slaten also brought up an old issue regarding Sales Tax Director Ed Sims, concerning confiscated guns, and the closure of substations by the Sheriff's Department.

Lyons Baker, a frequent critic of local government, said she has observed Shinn as counsel for the Decatur Board of Education.

"He does a poor job for them and as a taxpayer, I've been saying fire him all the time," Baker said.

file against the county. Also, Bartlett said Shinn is handling the situation with the federal court order to build a new jail.

Clark accused George of political grandstanding and said he was satisfied with Shinn's legal service.

Lyons, who was appointed to replace Glasscock when he won the chairmanship earlier this month, said he's known Shinn since 1966, and he believes Shinn has done a good job.

George said his main reason for changing lawyers is the way Shinn handled a situation more than two years ago with the garbage director's sister receiving seven years of garbage service free.

"He told her to pay it and pay it quickly and by doing that he went against the county," George said. "Another thing is that his law firm represents a lot of big businesses that come before this commission for tax abatements and that's a conflict of interest."

Shinn responded to George's comments and said he told the former garbage director's lawyer to get her sister to pay the money back. He said he believed it was his duty to do so, and he would do it again the same way.

Also, he acknowledged that his law firm represents a lot of businesses, but that any conflict of interest would not affect him because he is withdrawn from those matters.

"We're in the middle of a federal court order to build a jail and at this point it's not in the best interest to change attorneys," Glasscock said of his decision. "I think we need to be cautious about making any major changes."

Left Crooked for a reason!

George

Continued from page A1

Six months after the letter emerged, George questioned phone bills from the office of fellow Republican Amanda Scott, revenue commissioner, that showed 222 calls to Jackson County Revenue Commissioner Ron Crawford's office.

George, however, said his questions about the phone calls had nothing to do with the letter against him.

"I'm not going to get into name-calling because I have no proof, only speculation and I hold no grudges," he said. "I'm going to be in one of the political races and I will not get involved in murky waters with anyone."

Scott and her husband, state Republican Vice Chairman David Scott, had no comment.

Wood said he was not recruiting against George.

"This was a letter of invitation. I wanted to make sure that each district coming up had the very best that the Republican Party has to fill those positions and we may already have, that's not for me to say," Wood said.

Former TV news anchor Tom Kennemer, who is seeking the Republican nomination for District 4, said in December that Wood asked about his "political aspirations." Kennemer said he did not receive a letter.

Help with job description

The letter that went out for George's race gave specific details about the salary and benefits for the position, information that George said had to come from within the local government system.

"The salary for this office is $62,888 per year. A county vehicle is provided for the commissioner's use. Single or family health insurance coverage is available at an extremely attractive rate with Blue Cross/Blue Shield of Alabama. Retirement benefits are administered through the Retirement System of Alabama," the letter states.

Wood said he did not get the information from the County Commission office, but from another agency that he refused to name.

"The people in those positions have that information. I'm not going to say," Wood said.

George said he has a strong suspicion about who provided the information.

"It would have to be someone within the system for them to have details like that," George said. "It could very well be an elected Republican official."

Letters against Democrats

Wood said he also sent letters seeking candidates for the District 1 commission seat, which Don Stisher holds, and for District Attorney Bob Burrell's position. Burrell and Stisher are both Democrats.

"I didn't receive any response from those," Wood said. However, Wood's son David Wood plans to run for the Republican nomination for Stisher's job.

Initially Bill Wood said he had a copy of the letters for Stisher's and Burrell's races filed in his computer, but said he learned Tuesday afternoon that they had been deleted from the system.

Wood said he did not send a letter for the chairman's race.

"I just didn't," he explained.

Scott announced at one point that she was considering the chairman's race, but later said she would not run.

Wood's letter regarding George's position concludes, "Morgan County is in need of elected officials who will provide respectable leadership. Won't you please help today?"

Wood said that's no reflection on George's leadership.

"Like I said, I wanted to make sure we had the best candidates for each district. There's nothing between Stacy and I. If Stacy wins the nomination, I will get behind him 100 percent," Wood said.

While he has said he plans to seek re-election, George, 33, said he might consider other political options.

TRASH TO TREASURE OR IN THIS CASE JUST PUT IT IN THE TREASURY

My first day to serve as a county commissioner in Morgan County was interesting to say the least. I opened the door to the office at the district #4 shop in the Cotaco community and I saw one letter on the desk. The letter stated that the county commission would build a new jail, or the county commission would go to jail signed by U.W. Clemon (Federal Judge). I had not even reached the chair by the time I heard some mumbling. "There is some money in that top drawer of that desk in an envelope". As I looked inside, I saw around forty dollars and some change as I remember. I then ask, "Why is this money in the envelope here?" This was some of the scrap metal money from the last county clean-up. Immediately, I called the courthouse asking, "What do I need to do with this money from the scrap metal?" Our County Administrator instructed me to bring it to the next county commission meeting.

During the next couple of weeks, we made several hauls to the recycling plant ending up with just less than two-hundred dollars. At the commission meeting I reached in my pocket and dropped the money on the table by the microphone. Next, I simply said, "Here is the money from the scrap metal being sold to the recycling plant and from this day forward it needs to be written in check form". "The checks need to be written to the Morgan County Commission and put in a fund for District #4 use." As the change rolled around on the counter in front of me the rest of the commissioners went deathly quiet.

To my knowledge this was the first scrap metal money was ever brought to the Morgan County Commission to go into any legal fund. By the end of the year, we accumulated twenty-four hundred dollars from scrap metal. We used that money to chip-seal pave around one-half a mile of dirt road in the district that year and every year I served as the District #4 Commissioner. Over the eight years I served as county commissioner the total money for scrap metal was around twenty-thousand dollars. The moral to this story is a question. Who really knows how much money is being pocketed or misused by our elected officials? The answer is only GOD knows.

Trash to treasure is an easy lesson in accountability. While we hope our elected officials do the right thing when there is no paper-work necessary – scrap funds kind of wind up anywhere – enough scrap funds can pave many roads or help fund our elderly getting a hot meal.

To ensure accountability, receipts for all exchanges should be mandatory. For great accountability an independent auditor is a great start. Therefore, I think the elected State Auditor should be over the Examiners of Public Accounts. Just the thought that someone has the power to see what one is doing is usually enough to keep people honest. Someone not paid by – known of- related to – buddy of friend of a friend – who owes a favor, will look the other way (you get my drift).

One thing in this instance that helped a lot was me seeing my County Commissioner's job from the eyes of someone who had no political beholding to anyone. Observation taken by a person "not in the click" can do amazing things in government at a local, state, and federal level.

Just think, there are 67 counties in Alabama. I am only really discussing one. You can multiply the money stolen or misused by 67 and get a number that could decrease the amount of money you pay in the form of taxes. You could also use some of the money where the rubber hits the road literally. Our roads statewide could use some maintenance. I get tired of hitting potholes headed through Birmingham that result in a realignment of my vehicle. Under my watch it would not be as fun to be an elected official in Alabama.

Exodus 20:15 ESV

You shall not steal.

Dedicated to the growth and welfare of Morgan County

Hartselle Enquirer

Trash to treasure

Proceeds from scrap metal sale goes to pave roads

J.W. Greenhill
Hartselle Enquirer

Morgan County scrap metal is going to end up on the roads in District 4.

But don't worry about foreign objects on the roadway - the metal will be sold, with proceeds going to pay for paving material.

Commissioner Stacy Lee George said he will use approximately $2,400 obtained through the sale of scrap metal collected last fall to buy paving material for gravel roads in his district.

"This money will be used to chip-seal about one half mile of roads in District 4," George said. "That may not sound like much, but several of the roads we are working to pave are only two-tenths of a mile long," George said.

Approximately 17 miles of dirt and gravel roads remain to be paved in the eastern district of the county, he said.

George said the scrap metal was collected during last year's fall county clean-up day, when citizens were encouraged to bring old appliances and junk to the District 4 Shop.

The junk was sorted at the shop and the scrap metal later sold, George said.

"When I first took office, I found several checks from the sale of scrap metal and turned them into the general fund," George said.

Since learning more about the operation of the county, the District 4 commissioner said he found he could have used the funds in his district.

"We want to get the word out to people that bringing their junk to the district shop on clean-up days helps out," George said. "If people know, maybe they will bring more scrap metal to the shop and help us get the remaining unpaved roads surfaced quicker."

District 4 Commissioner Stacy Lee George stands amid a mound of scrap metal from culverts, old appliances and other items collected during county clean-up days. The scrap will be sold and the proceeds used to help pave rural roads in the district.

George to pave road with scrap money

By Sheryl Marsh
DAILY Staff Writer

Proceeds from the sale of metal that Morgan County residents dumped at the District 4 shop during a countywide cleanup will pay for paving one-half mile of a dirt road.

Commissioner Stacy George said his shop took in 89 tons of scrap metal and sold it for $2,400 to Tennessee Valley Recycling in Decatur.

"The money was collected from the spring cleanup and we just sold the last load of it. I plan to hand it over to the county administrator to go into my road building material fund. I will use it to buy chip seal to pave part of a dirt road," George said.

He said this could encourage more people to bring trash to the shop during cleanup days.

District 4 has 17 miles of dirt roads and George said he does not know which road will receive the paving.

The county has two annual cleanup days, one during the spring and the other in the fall. Residents take household items they want to discard to one of the shops. The items that District 4 received included bicycles, refrigerators, washers, dryers and golf clubs, George said.

"It made for a huge bundle of scrap metal and most of

Pave

Continued from page C1

the other stuff we took to the landfill for disposal," he said.

Currently, George said Morgan County Jail trusties are separating metal from items collected during the fall cleanup and he expects to make another profit.

"I estimate that we will get more than we did for the first. We might even get as much as $3,000 based on the size of the pile we have at the shop. Once they get finished, we'll sell it and put that money into the same fund to pave some more road," George said.

Commissioners Jeff Clark, Don Stisher and Faye Sparkman sold scrap metal, too, but they had a fraction of the tonnage that arrived at George's shop.

"Stacy's district takes in a lot more than we do and it's been that way," Clark said.

Clark received about $100 for scrap metal. Stisher got $213 and Mrs. Sparkman collected $420. They said they gave their money to County Administrator Willis Dockery to put into their budgets.

THE DECATUR DAILY

Riverfront/Classified

Lifestyles C3
Classified C8
Crossword C7

FRIDAY, FEBRUARY 9, 2001

Panel ends cash transactions

Morgan commissioners' new policy: checks only

By Sheryl Marsh
DAILY Staff Writer

The envelope stuffed with money looked suspicious.

County Commissioner Stacy George found it in a drawer at the Morgan County District 4 shop shortly after he took office.

He said it didn't make sense for a county shop to have cash from a business deal. So he took the envelope, containing about $427, to a County Commission meeting in November. He told fellow commissioners that he learned the money was a payment from a local business that bought scrap metal from the shop.

Commission Chairman Larry Bennich told George he should discuss it with County Administrator Willis Dockery, who would explain the situation.

George said Mr. Dockery told him that district shops receive scrap metal during annual countywide cleanup days, and they sell it to local dealers.

But his curiosity led to a change in the way all county shops will do business in the future. The shops will do no more cash transactions, according to commissioners, who said they want to avoid any appearance of impropriety.

Stacy George
Cash envelope triggers concern for commissioner

George said he told workers at his shop to request checks from Denbo Iron and Metal Inc. in Decatur rather than cash.

Joel Denbo, chief manager of operations, said the company can meet that request.

"We don't care one way or the other. It's just an easier transaction because we do a lot of small transactions. If they have no preference, depending on the size of the transaction and if it is within our policy threshold, we pay in cash. There's nothing diabolical in the transactions," said Denbo.

Mr. Dockery said the metal dealers give receipts with the cash payments, which show the weight of metal and the amount of money paid.

There is no law against counties receiving cash payments, a state official said.

"But any time an entity accepts cash, adequate procedures need to be in place to make sure the money is properly safeguarded. If none is in place, then that could cause problems," said Christine Harden, assistant director of the County Audit Division of the state Department

Please see Cash, page C2

Cash

Continued from page C1

of Examiners of Public Accounts.

George said it's safer to receive checks.

"I don't feel good about us handling cash. I just want to make sure we have a tight paper trail to show accountability for the taxpayers' money," he said.

District 2 Commissioner Faye Sparkman said she has requested checks for payment since she took office.

"I think it looks better and it helps you keep better records," Mrs. Sparkman said.

District 3 Commissioner Don Stisher and District 1 Commissioner Jeff Clark accepted cash payments from metal companies in the past, but both said they will start getting checks.

"That's the way it was done when I took over, and I just never changed it. But I tend to agree that check payments would be better," Stisher said.

Clark added, "Since there might be room for impropriety, I will start getting my workers to ask for checks when they make a sale."

ARE TAXPAYER PAID VACATIONS AT THE BEACH FOR WORK OR PLAY?

My family seldom went on vacations when I was a child. As I grew older it was still engrained in my head that extra money should not be spent on vacations. To this day it is still hard for me to plan a vacation. The way you are raised affects your personality for the rest of your life. As a county commissioner you are mandated to get a variety of classes through the Association of County Commissioners of Alabama in your first 2 years of office.

The first couple of weeks were flooded about travel times and places. The classes were set up through Auburn University and they ranged from Administration Management type courses all the way to abiding by Alabama Ethics Law. These classes usually take a couple of years to complete, and they are useful in your elected position. During my first two years on the commission, I always tried to get the closest classes to Morgan County, and I stayed away from the classes at the beach conferences. These commissioners and courthouse employees were in for a rude awakening because I was not molded in thinking the way they were.

I did not tend to go vacationing on my own money and I surely was not going vacationing on taxpayer money. I started questioning excessive travel after I decided to go on one of the beach trips to see if the trip was worth it. I witnessed many things that would make a taxpayer's blood boil. There is not enough ink to tell all the true stories in my head.

I had traveled several times to Washington DC by land and by air to see which was cheaper. I felt like anytime we were seeing our

United States Congressional members or United States Senators that was an important destination. I also felt our legislative trips to Montgomery, Alabama was important too.

Back to the beach trips, I ruffled feathers immediately when I told the courthouse I would not be staying on site at the conference location because it was too expensive. I stayed several miles inland and lodged for less than half of the cost as on the beach. The way these politicians and their courthouse friends get over on taxpayers is each person traveling is a member of an internal association usually a committee. This looks good on paper, and it is a smokescreen. The committees are the excuse used for early travel and this is the game being played.

The first day is almost always golf and I came prepared. I bought some used left-handed golf clubs a few months earlier and a basket of golf balls including a golf bag. The cow pasture beside my dad's home was the perfect driving range if the cows were not grazing. I did enjoy golf, but I preferred pitching horseshoes. The second day at the conference was a few break-out sessions, but nobody really went anywhere for real. People just seem to show their face and leave.

The night of the second day you could always count on a vendor having a room with free alcoholic beverages. Oh yes, there was gambling going on there too; the politicians were betting you taxpayers would never find out the real deal. The vendor was usually a large equipment provider for county government and the free drinks came with a price.

The next county commission meeting it appeared to me clearly. The courthouse cronies would push you to write the specifications so that the vendor would get the bid for large equipment purchases. Not me, I opened the specifications up so all legitimate bidders could bid; this ruffled more feathers.

The last day of the taxpayer paid beach trip we would have a social hour usually sponsored by an architect firm who would eventually be the architect firm hired to oversee new jails or courthouse annexes when they are built. Yes, we had to build a jail while I was on the Morgan County Commission, and I had to remind our chairman as well as the other commissioners that just because we received free shrimp as well as entertainment from a certain architect firm, we still must interview more providers. This stirred a lot of controversy because I said these things at public meetings.

The last order of business at the conference was all commissioners met and discussed how the Association of County Commissioners of Alabama can advocate additional taxes for additional revenue to spend. I found myself like little Johnny always raising my hand in opposition to the group. I was the only one raising my hand, but there were others that did not like what was being done. Now, I get back to Morgan County and the Decatur Daily calls me. The Decatur Daily asked, "What happened at the beach?" I started by saying, "it appears that Morgan County had roughly half of the Courthouse staff at the beach." Also, they are all sleeping in high priced lodging, and they are eating some real expensive food on the taxpayer dollar.

Later that year the Decatur Daily won an award for the coverage of the beach trip. I think you can see that I was not well liked by the other commissioners or the courthouse cronies. To throw salt on a wound, after returning from the taxpayer paid beach vacations some elected officials forgot to pay their travel advance back. When questioned about paying the money back there was a typical response and it sounded generic like this: "it was an oversight". Keep in mind every department head and elected official in the courthouse are a member of an association. This is the game used to take vacations on taxpayer money. I believe some travel is necessary in government. The only way to keep people honest in government is to monitor their activities and make their activities public. Perks of the position are a money grab for luxury and should not be tolerated.

One wonders about the mindset involved in thinking this is ok. I suppose if no one ever says anything and someone is a new attendee they perhaps "go with the flow." In the 8 years I served on the commission I saw things that would blow your mind. I saw in the archives of prior administrations travel receipts of one-hundred-dollar bills put on a copy machine and the copy was the receipt. I wonder why you would give a travel advance for 500 dollars in the form of a check and cash it when you have a county credit card in your pocket. Corruption is everywhere in your government.

Proverbs 22:16

He who oppresses the poor to increase his *riches,*
And he who gives to the rich, *will* surely *come* to poverty.

THE DECATUR DAILY

Sunday, September 8, 2002

Officials return beach allowances

Larry Bennich
[illegible]

By Sheryl Marsh
DAILY Staff Writer
[illegible] • 340-2437

After newspaper articles ran about a beach conference that Morgan County officials attended two weeks ago, Commission Chairman Larry Bennich and two commissioners returned all the money they got in advance for the trip.

Each of them received $300 for food and some other expenses for the conference, which was Aug. 19-22 at Perdido Beach Resort in Orange Beach, and returned the money about a week later.

THE DAILY contacted the commissioners while they were at the beach for a story about the trip.

▶Officials' expenses, A8

Please see Beach, page A8

List of beach expenses

Here's a list of the county employees and what they spent during a recent trip to a conference at Orange Beach:

▶Ed Sims, sales tax office director, got a $700 allowance and spent $1,081, will receive $381 reimbursement from county.

▶Judy Pope, sales tax office, got $700 advance, spent $1,072, will get $372 reimbursement.

▶O'Neal Terry, sales tax office, $700 allowance, spent $712.

▶Greg Bodley, (no allowance) spent $877 and county will pay reimbursement.

▶Brian Blanks, engineer's office, (no allowance) spent $823, will receive reimbursement.

▶James M. Kelley, engineer's office, (no allowance) spent $788 (includes mileage), will receive reimbursement.

▶Alphonso Patterson, sales tax office, $700 allowance, spent $693.

▶Brenda Blankenship, garbage/recycling coordinator, $800 advance, spent $558, returned $242.

Beach

Continued from page A1

Commissioners said, however, they did not return the money because of the news stories but because they didn't need to spend it.

The county sent 12 people to the Association of County Commissions of Alabama conference a week after commissioners warned local community service agencies and county departments to tighten their budgets.

Bennich returned $300 cash to the county Aug. 26. Commissioner Don Stisher wrote a $300 check dated Aug. 26 to the county's General Fund and Commissioner Jeff Clark wrote a $300 check that was dated Aug. 30, records show.

They said they did not eat at restaurants and that's why they did not spend the expense money. They used county-issued credit cards to pay for their rooms and gas.

In contrast to the commissioners, only two of the county employees who received an advance returned any money. One returned $7 and the other $242.

Bennich said the employees were invited to eat free food at the gatherings. He said he doesn't know why the commissioners ate the free food while the employees ate out at restaurants and charged it to the county.

"I can't answer that," he said.

In a letter to the editor in Wednesday's edition of THE DAILY, Clark said he spent $400 at the beach and returned all of his expense money.

Clark said later he did not mean to give the impression that he paid the money from his own pocket.

Also, he actually spent $271, rather than $400, according to county records.

"I charged the room and gas to my (county) credit card and I was rounding off what I spent when I said $400. I thought at first that the room was $199, but when I got the bill it was $109. The rooms were cheaper because we booked them early," said Clark, who spent two nights at the resort.

Stisher charged $242 to his county credit card for a two-night stay.

Bennich stayed three nights and charged $363 to his county credit card.

"I didn't spend any of the money because I didn't need to," he said of the $300 advance. "We always take it in case we need it for meals or anything like that."

He said he ate finger foods at the conference and one night he had dinner with the president of ACCA, who picked up his tab.

Clark and Stisher said extension service agents from several counties in the state cooked food and they ate those meals and finger foods at the conference.

Commissioner Faye Sparkman took a $500 advance and the county will reimburse her $37 for additional expenses.

Employees' bills

Eight county employees attended the conference with the commissioners and most of their individual bills were significantly higher than those of the elected officials.

The entourage included Ed Sims, director of the sales tax office and three of his employees; Brenda Blankenship, garbage/recycling coordinator; and Engineer Greg Bodley and two of his employees.

Some ate steak and eggs for breakfast, ribeyes and shrimp for dinner, and others either ate sandwiches or buffet food. Most of them gave $4 or $5 tips, charged to the county. Most of them slept in higher priced hotel rooms that cost from $129 to $189 per night and one employee stayed in a condominium that cost $135 per night and paid a $45 cleaning fee.

County Administrator Willis Dockery said the employees' rooms cost more because the employees did not make reservations in time to get the lower rates.

Blankenship was the lowest spender of the employees. She stayed three nights in one of the rooms that cost $109.

After learning about the individual expenses, District 4 Commissioner Stacy George, who complained that the group vacationed on taxpayers' money, called the expenditures ludicrous.

"Whew! It's awful and I don't believe any one of them would use their own money to pay high prices for lodging like that," George said. "We have got to cut out some of this waste. We've got to send less people on these trips like I brought up to them at budget hearings two weeks ago and didn't get any feedback.

"But, after finding out about all of this, I will revisit the situation and see if the other commissioners will support me in cutting out these frills."

Morgan sent more people to the conference than any of the most populated counties in the state. Jefferson County, for example, sent seven and Commissioner Betty Fine Collins said usually only commissioners attend ACCA conferences.

Morgan County commissioners said the trip was necessary and all 12 people received information at the conference that will help them in their work for the county.

Morgan cuts travel request by $70,000

By Sheryl Marsh
DAILY Staff Writer
sheryl@decaturdaily.com • 340-2437

Following an order to trim 10 percent from their budget requests, Morgan County officials cut almost $70,000 from their travel expenses for 2003, making it the lowest of the past four years.

County Administrator Willa Doss ery said some officials and their travel budgets voluntarily cut their

direct expenses after Chairman Larry Bennich instructed the heads to reduce their budgets about two weeks ago.

Bennich asked he decrease travel spending and others to trim the department heads to where to trim the cuts.

When County Commissioners testified, the total travel requests for 2003 last week, the amount was $598,347. After cuts, the travel budget is $528,387.

Morgan ponders travel, pay

By Sheryl Marsh
DAILY Staff Writer
sheryl@decaturdaily.com • 340-2437

Morgan County District 4 Commissioner Stacy George balked at a supervisor who asked for extra pay for two employees and an elected official who added raises for two workers in her office.

In addition to pay, George and the other commissioners scrutinized travel budgets for each department Tuesday during hearings for the fiscal 2005 budget.

Eddie Hicks, director of Emergency Management Agency, asked the commission to give 3 percent merit raises to Johnny Cantrell and Bill Thomson in addition to the 3 percent cost-of-living raise that all employees will get.

> "A four-door sedan would do just fine. The taxpayers don't take kindly to elected officials and employees driving these vehicles."
>
> **Stacy George**
> Says county officials shouldn't drive SUVs

DECATUR DAILY

Wednesday, August 28, 2002

Morgan led counties in officials at beach

County sent 5 more to conference than Jefferson

By Sheryl Marsh
DAILY Staff Writer
sheryl@decaturdaily.com

Morgan County sent more people to a conference at the beach last week than the largest counties in the state.

County Commissioner Jeff Clark, Don Stisher and Faye Spurlock and Chairman Larry Bennich, along with eight employees, attended an Association of County Commissioners of Alabama conference at Orange Beach. The four-day trip cost taxpayers about $18,998.

Officials in Jefferson and Mobile counties say they send a few representatives to conferences.

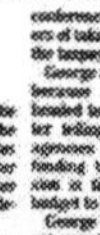

Beach trip comparison

Following is a comparison of Morgan, Limestone and Lawrence counties with several of the state's largest counties in population and representation at last week's conference at Orange Beach.

County	Population	No. at beach
Jefferson	662,047	7
Mobile	399,843	10
Madison	276,700	7
Montgomery	223,510	9
Shelby	143,293	11
Calhoun	112,249	7
Morgan	111,064	12
Limestone	65,676	8
Lawrence	34,803	5

Travel
Continued from page A1

Please see Travel, page A7

Please see Beach, page A5

Beach
Continued from page A1

DECATUR

Wednesday, August 21, 2002

Despite tight funds, Morgan sends dozen to beach meeting

Beach

THE SHERIFF OR THE SHARK (MONEY THAT IS)

In 2006 I made the worst tactical mistake of my political life. I decided to run for Morgan County Sheriff in between my county commission race. This issue with the sheriff, at the time, started with staffing issues at our new county jail. Later that week, after several heated public meetings, I paid the qualifying fee for Sheriff and the race was on. I had a very successful run for my second term on the county commission in 2004. I had two Republican primary candidates with one being a former news anchor in Huntsville and the other candidate was a former county commissioner's son-in-law, both well-funded. I won that County Commission Primary without a run-off and eliminated the Democrat in November to win a second term on the county commission.

The Scenario was simple but, the political run for sheriff was about to get complex. The first issue I brought up was simple; in a two-year period, the sheriff, at the time, pocketed approximately 104,000 thousand dollars from food money left over after feeding inmates. In this case he received one dollar and seventy-five cents per day per inmate from the State of Alabama for feeding inmates; any money left over according to Alabama state law can be kept as an addition to a sheriff's salary. I made the decision to run with no law enforcement experience and I was butchered up in the Republican Primary losing in a bad way. I did, however, bring up the issue of pocketing leftover food money during the primary that ultimately led to a Federal Judge putting the Sheriff in a Federal prison for twenty-four hours. The Federal Judge wanted to give our sheriff a literal taste of his own medicine; this referred to the Sheriff eating every meal then reporting back to court.

The problem the Morgan County Sheriff had dealing with feeding inmates is a clause in a federal court order stating the sheriff should adequately feed inmates. The Judge decided the inmates were not being adequately fed after the Sheriff fed them corndogs three times a day, and seven days per week for approximately three months. A trailer truck carrying corndogs turned over and our sheriff paid a small price (if any) for half of a trailer truck load full of corndogs. The other half of the corndogs was taken by the Limestone County Sheriff at the time. The moral to this story is greed landed this Sheriff in jail. No sheriff should ever have an opportunity to starve a person for a personal profit. Alabama is the only state in the United States that allows a sheriff to keep state money left over after feeding inmates. This issue is guarded by the strong Sheriff's Association in Montgomery. This law is unacceptable and must be changed in Alabama. This law was finally changed. The year is now 2021. Persistence does pay off. It just takes time so be patient. Publicity on an issue informs the public and in time change comes.

This is the story of desolation created in a simpler time which made way for a loophole allowing the less you feed the person detained – the more money (tens of thousands each year) goes into the Sheriffs pocket. Incentive to starve a person for a profit is plain wrong.

One can only imagine an Alabama's Sheriff's daily life in the mid and late 1930's, many times working ten or more hours with the chain gang. First, the ride to the work area, monitoring all day – then the ride back to the jail- then paperwork to fill out about the money left over from the feeding of the workers – the ride home – supper then do it again the next day.

It was with the idea in mind to not burden the sheriffs with this paperwork. A 1939 law allowed the sheriff of each county to keep the change – put it in their pocket – go about the rest of their day without the extra paperwork and be on his way home.

Greed is what eventually took over the hearts and souls of so many sheriffs in Alabama. The ways of creative food funds and making this pocketed amount grow are in the multitudes. At the time, a sheriff can house federal inmates for $3.00 - Feed them for $1.50 – pocket $1.50 per inmate each day for example – for as long as you can.

Think about this – when churches or those desiring to help sheriffs out by giving food happens that food represents money a sheriff no longer must come up with and can cause more to flow into his pocket. Fortunately, in the primary of 2018 several of the sheriffs accepting food money lost re-election.

I was excited when a new sheriff came to town in Morgan County. She was the first female sheriff ever elected in Morgan County. She was also the second in the state of Alabama and the first Republican female sheriff elected in history. Her first term was great and after reelection the temptation took over. In what could have gone down in history as a remarkable event simply ended in greed taking over.

I must add this in my book on 7/13/18 because our current Governor Ivey just took the first step in ending sheriffs keeping leftover state funded inmate food money. Governor Ivey did this by a stroke of a pen. She demanded that the $1.75 per day the state pays sheriffs cannot be put directly in the sheriffs' personal accounts. The money must be put in a government account and then dispersed. This is a big step that puts another action in place to keep the food money in a government account. The stage is set for our state legislature to fix this once and for all. Now, 105 State House members and 35 State Senators must act. They did act and this issue is finally resolved.

Proverbs 16:8

Better *is* a little with righteousness,
Than vast revenues without justice.

Hauled

Even if the food issue with Bartlett ends with him giving up the inmate money, other sheriffs, including Mike Blakely, will still be able to take advantage of the old state law while the Legislature looks on.

Nurses testified in Bartlett's defense, saying one of the inmates who lost about 30 pounds is in much better health for doing so.

The Decatur Daily

THE INDEPENDENT VOICE OF THE TENNESSEE VALLEY SINCE 1912

FRIDAY

Sheriff released from jail

Bartlett hauled in $668,722 in 6 years

Attorneys seek to stop Bartlett from taking food money

DECATUR DAILY

Tuesday March 28, 2006

Federal inmates here?

Sunday, March 26, 2006

THE DECATUR DAILY

No winners in shameful fight over jail staffing

U.S. District Judge U.W. Clemon two weeks ago held court in Decatur to settle the issue of how many jailers will staff the new Morgan County Jail.

He didn't side with Sheriff Greg Bartlett or with County Commissioner Stacy George, the two central figures in the on-going controversy.

The judge settled on 88, 16 more than Mr. George led the County Commission to approve and 14 fewer than the sheriff's scaled-back request.

Judge Clemon wasn't far down Interstate 65 on his way back to Birmingham before both sides claimed victory, with the sheriff saying the judge meant for him to have the 88 plus the nine dispatchers already on the payroll.

Not so, Mr. George said. Thus the judge had to revisit the issue in a written order issued last week. In essence, he said that 88 means 88, but he wasn't going to get involved in a dispatcher issue or in a local political battle. "In the outset, it is well to remind the sheriff and the commissioners that this court lacks both the inclination and the authorization to resolve political disputes," he wrote.

He emphasized that he wants the 2001 consent decree that led to building the new jail carried out to his liking.

The follow-up opinion last week is further rebuke of Morgan County government for not handling the matter in a reasoned manner. But he is leaving it to voters to make several key decisions about the participants. The sheriff challenged Mr. George to run against him in this year's Republican primary. Mr. George accepted, even if the sheriff was talking through his hat at the time, because incumbents usually don't openly invite opposition.

The feud probably cost both officeholders political capital. Whichever one wins the primary will face a Democratic opponent who isn't sullied by Daffy Duck, pig epithets and jail staffing.

The Decatur Daily

THE INDEPENDENT VOICE OF THE TENNESSEE VALLEY SINCE 1912

SUNDAY

Bartlett

Alabama Sheriffs Association Director Bobby Timmons said Morgan Sheriff Greg Bartlett's $95,000 take in unused prisoner food money last year is 'not unreasonable based on the fact that a sheriff in Mobile got $300,000.'

The Daily launched an investigation into Bartlett's inmate food money about three years ago after he refused to tell how much he was keeping. A 2006 audit that covered Bartlett's first two years in office showed he got $[illegible]. After *The Daily* discovered and disclosed the money, Bartlett stopped showing the amounts he kept in subsequent audits. He testified Wednesday that he kept $[illegible] in 2006, $[illegible] in 2007 and $[illegible] last year.

The Decatur Daily

EDITORIALS

Commission fumbles jail food proposal

The Morgan County Commission can attempt to rationalize the inmate food money that the sheriff pockets, but it can't escape the potential conflict of interest in the system.

A commission majority Tuesday refused to support a local legislative bill that would put the sheriff on salary only.

District 4 Commissioner Stacy George was the exception, although he preferred a lower salary.

Other commissioners' reasons for failure to support the bill were not supported by facts. District 2 Commissioner Ken Livingston said the bill would cost the county more money. District 1 Commissioner Jeff Clark said he has no problem with the state law that passed in 1939 that allows sheriffs to keep any amount of the state feeding allotment they don't spend.

District 3 Commissioner Kevin Murphy pulled a figure out of the air and said changing the system could cost the county "from $50,000 to $250,000."

State Rep. Ronald Grantland, D-Hartselle, said he had hoped the commission members would support his proposed bill that would set the sheriff's salary at $100,000 instead of $63,000 and send the leftover food money to the county.

They didn't, of course, and the potential conflict continues. The sheriff receives $1.75 per day per inmate for food. Sheriff Greg Bartlett listed his jail income for one two-year period as $104,000. State Examiners of Public Accounts later said he did not have to account for jail income, even though it comes from tax dollars. The most recent audit doesn't show the amount of leftover food money. The sheriff also is getting $3 per day to feed federal inmates now housed in the county's new jail.

The county commissioners and Chairman John Glasscock pride themselves on being good stewards of public money, yet they can find many reasons to support the status quo in this instance.

The only sound reason commissioners give for keeping the current arrangement is that it gives the sheriff incentive to watch his food budget.

The system should be changed statewide because of the potential for abuse. At a minimum, sheriffs should have to account publicly for these funds to make sure they feed inmates properly.

The Decatur Daily

Sheriff takes meal money; commissioners watch as legislator offers reward

To The Daily: Where is stealing — the unlawful taking of anything of value — not considered stealing? Oh, so you've noticed, too? And apparently you are right. It seems stealing is perfectly OK for politicians!

The latest glaring example of such ongoing travesty is Morgan County Sheriff Greg Bartlett stealing, of all things, lunch money. In movies or other fictional stories, the big bully forces smaller, more passive children to give him their lunch money or other things of value but, in the end, he is always caught and dealt with justly and properly.

But we're talking reality, not fiction; and it's been going on for a lengthy period. And to further the implication of politics, our glorious state Rep. Ronald Grantland, D-Hartselle, supports Mr. Bartlett in this illegal misuse of the people's money. When Mr. Bartlett ran for election to the position of Morgan County sheriff, he full well knew the pay that went with the job. But apparently he figured he could get himself a big bonus by taking money from the jail food account — and maybe elsewhere.

As a matter of routine, money is budgeted to feed all jail inmates and, I'm sure, this is done as a line item. That being the case, any use of these funds other than that for which it was intended is a misappropriation of funds. And Mr. Grantland proposes not only not to penalize/punish the thief, but to actually reward him by retaining him and increasing his pay?

Should theft, its accomplices and its supporters be rewarded or punished? It is our money.

Where are our county commissioners, our leaders? Are they part of the problem? It's apparent they certainly are not a part of the solution. Maybe it is time more attention and support were paid District 4 Commissioner Stacy George.

James L. [illegible]
Hartselle

George right, Bartlett wrong on jail staffing

THE DECATUR DAILY

Plain and simple: Sheriff Greg Bartlett is a jerk. We need more Stacy Georges. It's a delight to read about what he does and says. He calls it like most of us see things.

The County Commission says it will add staff as needed and I believe it will. Why should Bartlett get the staff now?

Brenda Coburn
Decatur

THE GARBAGE DIRECTOR SCANDAL; A TRASHY, BUT TRUE STORY

I found out quickly in politics, if you are willing to confront corruption and misuse of funds there are people within the system that will send you tips continuously. There are many whistleblowers in government, but they normally want to remain anonymous. As for me, I just broadcasted things the people should know about in their local government at our county commission meetings every two weeks. I remember the day I watched a Morgan County Garbage truck drive into Marshall County and pick up some garbage. I had a tip that our garbage director's sister was getting free garbage pick-up in another county. As the garbage truck stopped to pick up the garbage, I snapped a picture for evidence. I immediately started my research to get a timeline of exactly how long this had been taking place. The research proved the residence was her sister and she had been receiving the service free approximately 7 years.

I have never witnessed such an effort to cover something up or disprove something in my life. The chairman of the county commission directed some private surveyors to survey the county line. They tried over and over to move the Morgan/Marshall County lines, but all efforts fell short. I found out firsthand that most of the time in politics the cover-up is worse than the crime. As I researched this issue further, I thought of something else that might be of some use. In the early 2000's cell phones were still somewhat expensive. I knew the area in eastern Morgan County as well as western Marshall County was on the Brindlee Mountain phone network. This was a small network that was long distance to call the Morgan County District #4 Shop, Hartselle, and Decatur. The garbage department was in Hartselle, and I knew that was long distance to call. I had an 800 number at my shop, and I thought maybe the garbage director had an 800 number too. Those 800 numbers were popular back in those days because cell phones were just getting started and most cell phone plans had a maximum number of minutes available. I suspected the Garbage Director would say she had no contact with her sister at work; after I looked through the phone records, I saw over a hundred dollars' worth of calls from not only the sister in Marshall County, but a lot from her other sister in Georgia.

To shorten this story, I immediately filed an Ethics Complaint with the Alabama Ethics Commission in Montgomery on both free garbage and personal abuse of the 800 number for personal gain. Next, the 7 years of free garbage was paid; this payment took the criminal element out of the Ethics Complaint Filing since it was paid back plus interest. However, the phone bill was not paid and several months later the Alabama Ethics Commission found the Garbage Director guilty on an ethics charge for using the 800 number for personal gain. The result was a firing of the Garbage Director as well as the Ethics Violation on the phone calls. I often say to people, "If the people knew everything, I have witnessed there would be a demand to remove most of the people in power at the Morgan County Courthouse (politicians, department's heads, and some other employees.)"

The key to good government is people in power knowing that someone is watching their actions. Think about this, the only thing that keeps anyone honest is fear of something. I fear GOD, but some people have no fear. These people with no fear are dangerous individuals and must be closely monitored. Some people cannot handle power; this situation is a good example of someone who cannot handle power.

Now, we come to another valuable lesson in dealing with corruption - The attempted cover-up. When you know it happened, you watch the perpetrator, and you see their cohorts gathering to circle the wagon it is interesting to see the roaches run from the light.

Get the basic hard-core evidence first thing. Take pictures – get paperwork – all of it you can do before involving anyone else. One never knows who is going to be circling the wagon later. The faster you can figure out who is covering for the crook the faster you can connect them together. At that point the politicians will cut and run if they can.

Next, have your information thorough and exact. You need to know where your county lines are in this case. No arguing or fussing – state the facts – as many as you truly have and look for any overlooked means of proof. In this case the wrong doer will usually shake their head side to side and hold their head down in shame.

Leviticus 19:11

'You shall not steal, nor deal falsely, nor lie to one another.

TRASH PICKUP IN QUESTION

George claims garbage director providing free service for sister

LEAVING MORGAN COUNTY

THE DECATUR DAILY

RIVERFRONT

Wednesday, March 19, 2003

Blankenship hearing today

Meeting closed to attorneys; George does not want garbage workers pressured

DECATUR DAILY

Saturday, March 15, 2003

Trash director's sister pays

Morgan accepts $766.91 from Marshall resident

Ethics panel to investigate Blankenship garbage case

By Sheryl Marsh

Blankenship to stay on job during investigation

Morgan garbage coordinator allegedly gave free service to sister

By CHANDLER NATHERNANT
The Arab Tribune

Read
The Arab Tribune

JESUS CHRIST IS THE ANSWER

Jesus Christ is the Answer #1

George out to get Blankenship

THE DECATUR DAILY

Blankenship still has job?

THE DECATUR DAILY

DECATUR

Friday, March 7, 2003

Trash

Garbage

Continued from page 4A

Employee: Pickup made him curious

By Sheryl Marsh

DECATUR DAILY

Monday, April 14, 2003

Morgan fires garbage director

Garbage

"It was one of any other citizen we would be fired and put in jail for stealing."

County replacing Shinn in Blankenship case

Stacy George said Attorney Bill Shinn's questioning left him wondering if he was trying to get to the truth or find someone innocent.

Shinn told Marshall resident to pay fee

DECATUR DAILY

Tuesday, April 15, 2003

Blankenship can appeal firing

Commissioners vote 2-1 to remove garbage director

DECATUR

Sunday, March 30, 2003

Documents raise questions about garbage job hiring

THE DECATUR DAILY

Ethics violation finding should put others on notice

Hiring

"That thing is turned over to the Ethics Commission and I don't think it's appropriate for me to do any more talking about it."

THE DECATUR DAILY

RIVERFRONT B1

Bennich backs Blankenship

Chairman: 'Brenda has done an outstanding job of running this department'

THE DECATUR DAILY

RIVERFRONT C1

CLASSIFIED

Blankenship appeals

Former garbage director requests Personnel Review Board hearing

DECATUR DAILY

Thursday, August 5, 2004

Blankenship: Minor violation

Ex-garbage director faces telephone fine

Morgan hires ex-prosecutor for hearing on Blankenship

Fine

Garbage

State ethics panel to hear Blankenship testimony

DECATUR DAILY

Wednesday, April 9, 2003

Free calls linked to Blankenship's sisters

Garbage director's firing is upheld

Trash

REVENUE COMMISSIONER: "I AM HEADED TO JACKSON"

This reminds me of a Johnny Cash song called Jackson. 'I'm goin' to Jackson' is the start of the song. The actual problem is when you return from Jackson or any travel for Morgan County in your appointed or elected status you need to pay your travel advance back providing receipts for the expenses within 7 days. The travel scandal turned up because of sifting through excessive phone calls between the Morgan County Revenue Commissioner and the Jackson County Revenue Commissioner. What are excessive calls? The total number of phone calls from the two Revenue Commissioners was approximately four hundred calls within one year's time. This totals almost two-hundred dollars of calls between the two revenue Commissioners for the year.

This phone issue does not exist today because of a single monthly cost for unlimited phone calls. In the year 2000 cell phones and hardline phones were billed long distance charges. My thought was if they are calling maybe they are traveling too. The Revenue Commissioner in Morgan County during this time was a Certified Public Accountant (CPA) who failed to pay back several travel advances and the excuse was simple," It was just an oversight." In politics you hear this excuse a lot, especially when money is missing; they reconcile the money quickly after they are caught to take out any criminal element.

There were several travel advances that were almost a year late on their return. The sad part is if this issue had not been made public this money would have never been returned. One travel advance was eight-hundred dollars and nearly one year later four-hundred sixty-four dollars of the travel advance was returned.

She provided receipts for the remainder of the money. Next, a two-hundred-dollar travel advance was over one year past due when returned. Lastly, there were two more travel advances for five-hundred dollars each returned. These travel advances were from the previous year. What a mess and nobody caught it until the digging started.

The moral to this story is without oversight-politicians, political appointments, etc. do what they want to do; they do this without fear most of the time. It takes a politician the first few years to learn what he or she is doing. In about five or six years of service you get the legal things done that you promised to do at least on a local level. After the end of 7 years, you know exactly how to steal money. I suggest term limits with no elected official serving more than twelve years although I would recommend eight years. This is from a city council, school board, county commissioner, judge, district attorney, state house member, state senate member, United States House member, United States Senate member, etc. My slogan in 2000 was, "Clean house from the courthouse to the Whitehouse"; this slogan can be used for term limits as well. In politics any politician can be replaced; your city, county, or state will not miss a beat I promise no matter how important they think they are.

Oversight is the key here. You always must watch politicians because they tend to use taxpayer money different than their own. "If it is done in the dark, it must be brought to the light and if it survives in the light, it is probably alright." Stacy Lee George (John 1:5)

Proverbs 12:22

Lying lips are an abomination to the LORD,
but those who act faithfully are his delight.

George questions 225 telephone calls made from revenue office

By Sheryl Marsh
DAILY Staff Writer
smarsh@decaturdaily.com • 340-2437

After checking phone bills of all departments and finding more than 200 calls to Scottsboro's Morgan County District 4 Commissioner Stacy George said the county should implement an accountability procedure.

The bills were not labeled by department, just numbers, so George said he did not know which office the calls were made from or who made the calls.

The courthouse phone register shows the calls came from Revenue Commissioner Amanda Scott's office.

THE DAILY checked with the Jackson County Commission office and learned that the Scottsboro number is the direct line to Jackson County Revenue Commissioner Ron Crawford's office.

Phone records show that one or more people made 225 calls from the Morgan office to Crawford's office between August 2002 and August 2003. Some calls lasted 57 minutes. All of the calls amounted to about $100. The county pays a cents-a-minute for long-distance calls.

"Since the actual calls tell how numbers involved in the situation last year with our garbage department work," George said, "I've been trying to do maintenance, feeling it ways we can save money at least sure there's no kind of abuse of phone lines going on."

Stacy George
Decide a commissioner questioned number

Amanda Scott
Morgan County revenue commissioner

Please see Calls, page A8

Jackson County Commission Chairman James E. Tidmore, left, warned Revenue Commissioner Ron Crawford not to answer questions about hundreds of phone calls involving Morgan County.

Sunday morning, March 14, 2004

Calls

Continued from page A1

Last year, records showed that someone received more than $1,300 worth of phone calls on the toll-free line in the garbage department and some calls lasted an hour or more.

George said the Scottsboro calls got his attention.

"I just pulled all phone records from AT&T and the abundance of calls to Scottsboro stood out," George said. "It prompted me to ask our county administrator to send a letter of memo to all department heads and elected officials asking them to do maintenance on phone calls to make sure the error number is not showing up one-plus times in a year.

"This is not aimed at anyone. It's just a good business

tool to use and I think it would be good if we exercised it. If we is it right, we would be surprised on how much we are taxpayers," George said.

Scott and Crawford both said the number of calls came because they were involved with social photography technology for their offices.

Scott said she and her other appraiser, Richard Gattis, consulted with Crawford's office concerning the project.

"We were involved members of the same team with Atlantic Technology, the company that developed the property in our county," Scott said.

She said the calls were an increase because the project, which entailed photographing all parcels in the county, was so detailed. She said she made Jackson County to entertain cuts with about the project. "We know they were working on the same project at the same time and it was a big help to me over here."

Crawford said the project required lots of calls.

"It's a complicated process. I don't understand it all," he said.

Crawford said he talked to Gattis and Fields sometimes.

Scott said Jackson is not the only revenue office she called.

"I called other offices, too, but they probably don't show up because they're not long distance. It just so happens that at the particular time Jackson County had the same project going on," she said.

Scott said other counties were doing aerial photography but at different times.

Crawford said the records contain lots for a year or more and it was justified for him.

"It was before we saw lots a year ago with the garbage

In addition to herself, Scott and Gattis, her chief clerk Renee Fields and others in the office also called Scottsboro, sometimes about various subjects.

"It's real common to call and see how other counties handle things like tax exemptions in all are governed by the same state laws," Scott said.

Fields said she and her only revenue officer she called.

Fields and she called the office for one of Crawford's employees who does bookkeeping sometimes because they are of the same software system.

George said his search did not show a great number of long-distance calls to other offices, but he will continue to monitor phone records periodically.

"Just to make sure we don't get surprised like we did once a year ago with the garbage

this and it was a big help to me over here."

Crawford said the project required lots of calls.

"It's a complicated process. I don't understand it all," he said.

Crawford said he talked to Gattis and Fields sometimes.

calls because they were much as aerial photography programs at the same time and swapped information.

Fifty-one of the calls were less than a minute long, suggesting that the parties did not connect or left messages rather than having a conversation.

115 calls from Scottsboro

Crawford used his county phone to make 115 phone calls to Decatur, including a couple the day before Valentine's Day in 2003 to candy shops.

Crawford said he checked on candy prices because he was probably thinking about buying some for his wife or Valentine's Day but decided against it.

"I heard that the candy was good," he said.

Most of the calls were to Scott's office for business reasons, he said.

A majority of the calls came between August and August 2003, the time they said they were discussing the project.

The calls centered after the project's completion, but decreased in frequency. Morgan County records show that 25 calls were made to Scottsboro in months after August 2003.

But Fields's December and phone bill, the latest available, showed no calls to Scottsboro.

Scott said the other people she called, Atlantic Technology, but he had the company to do aerial photography to use in mapping the tax purposes.

Cell-phone calls

Scott called Scottsboro 35 times from her county cell phone.

Most calls to Crawford's number were at 4 p.m. on Nov. 5, 2003, election night.

Scott said she has already explained that all the calls were for business and she has nothing further to say.

Crawford's explanation for the after-hours calls was: "To wife they were concerning the project. I don't know I may have asked her about it. (She

project."

His phone records show that he called other revenue commissioners throughout the state, including DeKalb County, which also was working on an aerial photography project. He called that office about 18 times, according to county records.

The project

Minutes from a Jackson County Commission meeting show that Crawford got authorization for the project Dec. 10.

He and Scott said they started discussing the project in August 2002 and it lasted through August 2003.

Morgan County Commission records show the county received a contract with Atlantic for Scott's office and for county engineers in March 2003.

Crawford said all communication was necessary to carry on the project. "It's pretty complicated stuff."

"That's the biggest project our county has ever been involved in and we kind of bounced our office after Morgan County because I got in proceed with their office," he said.

Morgan County Engineer Greg Bodley said the aerial photography is detailed.

"Amanda did the flying portion and we piggy-backed at what she was doing," Bodley said.

"It is an involved process. What they've done is photographed maps to be... pieces," Bodley said.

The county will use the data we as a base for tax mapping...

to assist with assessing property, according to Bodley.

After two DAILY reporters obtained the phone records in Scottsboro, Jackson County Commission Chairman James Tidmore confronted them in front of Crawford.

Tidmore warned Crawford not to answer any more questions about the calls.

Then Tidmore told the reporters to "hit the door."

Please see Calls, page A7

Morgan-to-Jackson calls total nearly 400

By Sheryl Marsh
DAILY Staff Writer
smarsh@decaturdaily.com • 340-2437

Almost 400 phone calls occurred between the offices of Morgan County Revenue Commissioner Amanda Scott and Jackson County Revenue Commissioner Ron Crawford within a year.

The calls totaled 62 hours, and cost Morgan $149 and Jackson $651, according to phone records that THE DAILY researched.

The combined total of 397 calls is 172 more than the 225 from Scott's office that Morgan County District 4 Commissioner Stacy George questioned during a recent meeting.

"I can't make the determination as to whether or not the phone calls were business. I have to assume that they were, and if they are, that's fine," George said after learning of the additional number. "We are adamant. It's just something that elected officials and department heads need to continue to monitor."

Both Scott and Crawford said they exchanged numerous

Revenue head questions District 4 toll-free calls

By Sheryl Marsh
DAILY Staff Writer
smarsh@decaturdaily.com • 340-2437

After Morgan County Commissioner Stacy George questioned 225 phone calls between Revenue Commissioner Amanda Scott and Jackson County Revenue Commissioner Ron Crawford, Scott is now questioning calls to a toll-free line from George's District 4 shop.

Scott faxed copies and had her chief clerk deliver copies of phone records to THE DAILY and wants that showed someone called the county shop toll-free line 225 times from Gadsden during 2002 and 2003.

She said there was nothing wrong with the calls to get back at her fellow Republican for questioning her phone bills.

"I would hope they're not doing this," she said. "B. just concerned our shop on county phone calls were originating from Gadsden."

The calls are from different numbers. Many are business numbers, while others are no longer in service. The calls are not to George's direct line.

George: Calls checked

George said he was aware of the calls and showed THE DAILY documentation that reports that he had been checking on the Gadsden calls since last year.

"I raised the numbers and a lot of them were a bunch and no issued since company," George said.

THE DAILY confirmed that some calls were from South Trust Bank, HealthSouth and Weaver Insurance in Gadsden. Some of the other Gadsden numbers were no longer in service.

One of the numbers is the exact number of Pete Burgess, a manager of commercial accounts at the bank. Burgess said George called her last year inquiring about who had

been calling the toll-free number.

"He called several months ago, probably closer to a year ago, and said my number kept showing up in the bill there, and I told him as far as I know I had never dialed down there, because I don't even know anybody in Morgan County," Burgess said.

The longest call lasted 11 minutes and cost $1.48. The total for all the calls was $76.

Secretary investigated -

George said the Gadsden calls seemed to have stopped, but now he cannot enter another code running in on the line and had his secretary, Vic Copeland, check some of those calls. Current phone bills show no Gadsden calls to the shop.

Copeland said she checked numbers from Jasper that appeared on the latest phone bill.

"I brought the calls to Stacy's attention because I do the bills. I checked one Jasper number and it was to a residence and another one was to a doctor's office," Copeland said.

She said the people with whom she spoke did not know how their numbers got on the shop phone bill because they said they had never called there.

THE DAILY checked one of the Jasper numbers, and it is the office of Dr. Roy Sims.

George said he talked with his employees and asked them if they knew who was receiving calls from people on the line.

"I had a meeting with all employees and told them that if anybody was playing around on the toll-free line they need to stop it," George said.

New toll-free plan?

George said he talked with a telephone company official who came up with another plan for the toll-free line, which he will present to the County Commission at the next meeting.

Scott said she did not search George's phone records, but someone gave them to her; however, she refused to give

the person's name and phone number.

"I'll have her call you," she said.

Nothing to hide

George said he doesn't mind Scott or anyone else questioning his records because "I have nothing to hide. I don't use my office for personal gain in any way."

"One thing for sure is that none of the calls are from cell-phone ... like those that we were involved in the line of calls between Mrs. Scott's office and Mr. Crawford's office," George said.

Crawford made 115 calls to Decatur, including two to candy shops in Decatur, records showed. When questioned more than a month ago, Crawford said he asked the Decatur candy shops a day before Valentine's Day but because he was thinking about buying candy for his wife.

Phones to travel

Scott said his search of phone records led him to travel records.

"Once I saw all the phone calls to Scottsboro, I looked to see if there had been any trips to Scottsboro and there were two where Mrs. Scott charged the county for mileage last year," George said.

Records show that Scott claimed mileage for a trip to Jackson County on May 1, 2003, and Scott later that the reason for the trip is "meeting, Jack and County area." The reason she gave for a trip to Scottsboro on Aug. 8, 2003, was "GIS meeting."

Scott said Friday that she had already explained that she and Crawford discussed aerial photography in phone conversations and the meetings were about that subject.

Collectively, there were 83 hours of phone conversation between her office and Crawford's. Also there were 180 calls between the two offices, including calls to cell-phone records according to phone records

project."

His phone records show that he called other revenue commissioners throughout the state, including DeKalb County, which also was working on an aerial photography project. He called that office about 18 times, according to county records.

THE DECATUR DAILY

Scott pays back year-old advance unused for travel

By Sheryl Marsh

Morgan County Revenue Commissioner Amanda Scott waited more than a year to return an unused travel advance when county policy requires her to return the money within seven days.

In addition, she reconciled two other travel advances Monday for trips she took almost a year ago, records show.

A state examiner said the tardy reimbursements are unacceptable.

Last month, THE DAILY reported that on March 12 Scott reimbursed the county $466 from an $866 advance she received Jan. 26 of this year.

Amanda Scott
Morgan revenue commissioner

▶ Scott questions District 4 toll-free calls. A6

Other records show that she received an advance for $886 Feb. 2, 2003, and she reimbursed the county for the total amount March 12 of this year. County Administrator Willie Dockery said Scott repaid the entire $886 because she did not have receipts from the trip.

Scott gave Dockery a check Monday to reimburse the county for two advances she got last year. She received one for [illegible] May 28 and one for [illegible] July 13.

She paid $113 to the county for the July advance, which she said included 3 percent interest, and $116.27 for the May advance, which included 3 percent interest.

Please see Scott, page A6

Scott

Continued from page A1

Records show that the money she used was for mileage to Gulf Shores and for food. She attended conferences each time, according to records.

Scott, who is a certified public accountant, said her failure to reconcile all the advances was an oversight and she paid 1 percent interest for each month the money was not paid. She said she also planned to pay 12 percent interest on the year-old $886 advance.

"I inadvertently failed to reconcile advance travel and I appreciate Mr. Dockery for calling this to my attention," she said in a prepared statement.

A year too late

Randy O'Bannon, an auditor for the state Department of Examiners of Public Accounts, said the state provided guidelines for all counties to follow concerning travel advances.

"They are supposed to provide receipts and settle up within a reasonable time. If they are owed money they should receive it, and if they owe money they should reimburse the county," said O'Bannon. "That's basic accounting. One reason why they should pay as quickly as possible is because people have a tendency to lose receipts.

"Our office furnished guidelines to all county commissions that suggested a format on how to account for travel advances when the Legislature first passed an act to allow such advances. From an accountant's standpoint, I would expect these things to be settled within a week after returning from a trip, especially if the county is owed money. I will definitely be looking at this because a year late is just not acceptable."

District 4 Commissioner Stacy George raised questions during a commission meeting about Scott's travel advances. The county has a policy that requires officials and employees to return any unused advance money within seven days after they return from a trip.

George proposed that the commission pass a resolution to impose interest on unreconciled advance money, but a motion failed with no votes from Chairman Larry Bennich, District 1 Commissioner Jeff Clark and District 3 Commissioner Don Stisher.

New system

After learning about the most recent reimbursements Scott made for advances last year, Bennich said changes have been made.

"Mr. Dockery has put a system in place where they're going to keep a log on advances," Bennich said. "We're going to try to watch it a little closer and make sure it doesn't happen again. It's something that's approved in their budgets, and people need to be responsible for taking care of their business. But if they don't, we're going to try to bird dog a little bit."

Dockery said she started bringing Scott's outstanding advances to her attention in early March and that since that time she has told the accounts payable officer to give Dockery reports of all advance pay records so that she can keep up with the situation for all departments.

Accounts reconciled

A search of travel records for other officials — including Bennich, all four commissioners, the deputy county administrator, the license commissioner, the sheriff, the transportation director, the sales tax director and Dockery — shows that all their advance travel was reconciled.

Commissioners had varying opinions about the situation.

"If someone knowingly and willfully tried to keep county money for a year that's a problem, but if it was an oversight it's different," Clark said.

Stisher said he leaves such matters up to the department head.

"Amanda is accountable to the people who elected her, and I think she is accountable to her office," he said.

District 2 Commissioner John Glasscock and George both said the commission needs to make changes.

"A travel advance for county employees or officials should not be outstanding a year," said Glasscock. "I think it would have to be extreme, extenuating circumstances like a tragedy for someone to keep money out for a year. A change is needed, and one idea I have is that if a person has an outstanding unsettled advance, they shouldn't be granted another one until it's settled."

Interest payment sought

George said he agreed with Glasscock's suggestion but he still favors paying interest.

"I feel like until we put procedures in place to stop these oversights, it will be hard to build the public's confidence in local government," George said.

"The only way to stop it is to have it filed separately until the unpaid balances are paid. I proposed a penalty of interest, and it failed. I would be willing to revisit that and work with the commission on coming up with a penalty after seven days."

JESUS CHRIST
IS THE ANSWER
Jesus Christ is the Answer

THE DECATUR DAILY

Morgan travel questions rile Bennich

By Sheryl Marsh

▶ Commissioner quiet on secretary's resignation. C1
▶ Meeting synopsis. A4

It was another contentious meeting Monday for the Morgan County Commission, with a confrontation between Chairman Larry Bennich and District 4 Commissioner Stacy George over spending for travel and mileage reimbursement.

George made a motion to penalize elected officials and employees who do not refund the county from unspent travel advances within seven days as required by a current resolution.

District 1 Commissioner Jeff Clark asked specifically to whom George was referring.

George said he had a printout from the commission office that showed several people received travel advances and some of them have not returned money left over from their trips.

Please see Travel, page A7

Travel

Continued from page A1

After the meeting, George said he wanted to question Revenue Commissioner Amanda Scott about her travel expenses, but Bennich cut him off before he had a chance.

Bennich said George's actions were "political."

"If I had the opportunity to conclude my questioning of Mrs. Scott, I could have asked her about why she refunded the county in March for a trip she took in January," George said. "This is one of the examples of returning unused travel money."

The record George has shows that Scott received an $866 advance Jan. 26, but waited until March 12 to reimburse the county $466 left over from the trip.

"From that you can see that all these questions were legitimate," George said. "Mr. Bennich can holler political all he wants to, but the people of this county should not be responsible for supplementing salaries through mileage. And when officials and employees go on beach conferences, the taxpayers shouldn't have to pay for the family to go play putt putt golf," George said.

District 2 Commissioner John Glasscock seconded George's motion to charge interest on money not paid back beyond seven days.

Clark and District 3 Commissioner Don Stisher voted against it. Bennich voted no to break the tie and defeat the motion.

Later, Clark said he is not against the resolution, but he did not have enough information.

Stisher said he voted against it because of the county's existing requirement that employees reimburse the county within seven days after travel.

George also talked about officials and employees who charge mileage for local travel, saying they should use county vehicles, if they have them in their departments.

George said Scott has vehicles assigned to her department and so does Sales Tax Director Ed Sims.

Stacy George
Morgan County commissioner

Larry Bennich
Commission chairman

Bennich told George he should ask Scott and Sims about the matter in private rather than bring it up at a public meeting.

Scott was present, however, and answered questions about her employees driving personal vehicles. She noted that her department has three vehicles, but they are so old that she should ask for new ones. She said the 37.5 cents the employees receive per mile does not compensate for the wear and tear on their personal vehicles.

Bennich intervened before George could finish questioning Scott.

"I know why you're asking these questions," Bennich said. "It's political and I'm tired of listening to this crap."

Then, George proceeded to question Sims.

Sims said he does not collect local mileage and his employees with county vehicles use them to conduct license inspections.

Bennich cut off the questioning and adjourned the meeting.

After the meeting

George said if Bennich had let him finish, he would have shown a pattern of possible abuse of mileage collections or at least officials could have explained it. As for Sims, George said he understands that his employees need the vehicles in their line of work, but they should not be allowed to take them home.

"They should be parked at the end of the day," George said.

He said he has a printout of local mileage that shows Scott and two revenue employees received $4,873 for mileage last year. The records also show that Chief Appraiser Richard Gattis and other appraisers collected mileage, although they have access to county vehicles.

Scott received more than half of the money.

"I wanted to ask her how much of the mileage was local because it appears that most of it is for within the county," George said. "It looks like a salary supplement to me."

In addition to the mileage, George said he planned to question why Gattis has a county vehicle while he lives in Madison County.

Efforts to contact Scott later were unsuccessful.

Post-meeting dispute

George, who has questioned travel and other records from the time he went into office four years ago, sparked fire from Bennich, who confronted him after the meeting.

"I'm tired of you using this podium for political reasons," Bennich told George.

"Larry, you've announced that you're not running anyway, so I don't know why you're so upset about what we're trying to accomplish," George responded.

"I'm concerned because you are trying to tear down what I've built up with employees," Bennich said.

Later George said, "I have no intentions of changing my beliefs that there are certain issues the public should be aware of, especially when their money is involved. I work for the people, not for Larry Bennich."

Turmoil between the commission's Republican and Democratic members continues as the June political primaries approach. George is seeking reelection, but faces opposition from some leaders in his own party. Clark, a Democrat, and Glasscock, a Republican, are both running for Bennich's job. Stisher, a Democrat, is seeking re-election.

Scott and George are both Republicans, but this is the second time George has raised questions about spending in her office.

A committee of unnamed Republicans agreed to seek a letter seeking candidates to run against George. Scott would not comment about the political move and George would not say whom he believes is involved.

WHAT IS MORGAN COUNTY AREA TRANSPORTATION SYSTEM (MCATS) FOR?

If I remember it correctly it was hot and close to the fourth of July. Little did anyone know, but the fireworks were about to go off in Morgan County again. I remember the day James Cooper called me like it was yesterday. James Cooper was a war veteran who I had known for several years. He was always concerned about the Florette area whether it was drainage issues or politicians stealing money. Sometimes stealing can be called misuse of tax dollars at least when the politicians get caught or they call it an oversight.

James Cooper said, "be at Jacks restaurant at the corner of highway 67 and highway 36 early in the morning about daybreak." As I arrived James said, "George, have a seat here and tell us what the heck is going on in that shopping center across the road?" As I sipped that warm cup of coffee, I watched patiently across Highway 67. It was like a movie is the best I could describe it or a community stakeout. "Here they come," James said; my heart was pounding like I had just sprinted at the end of a long run when they pulled in the parking lot across the road from the restaurant. I watched as several people jumped out of the Morgan County Area Transportation System bus, and the people dispersed in several directions. I noticed the vehicles they were getting in, and these vehicles were mostly nice SUV's including full size pick-up trucks too. All these vehicles looked much better than the bus they piled out of. Next, another group of people immediately got in the bus. The bus did not stay long, and it was like dust in the wind. I attempted to follow it, but by the time I drove over to parking lot everyone was gone including the bus. I immediately headed to the county shop and called the MCATS director. She said, "Oh that is just my guys going to the Good Year Plant in Gadsden." She basically described this as a pilot program done through the State of Alabama. I automatically called the courthouse and put the item on the next work session agenda to discuss at our next county commission meeting.

We had several public hearings, and it was calculated the riders paid $20.00 per week for two groups of eight. The amount of money received from the riders barely covered the fuel cost. My position was if there were elderly individuals in Morgan County with a need to get their medications, we could only use MCATS buses for our population in need. In addition, if we cannot provide this service to people driving to Birmingham and Huntsville then we cannot participate in this program. My opinion was the program was not advertised and it was given to a chosen group of people. The program was stopped and to my knowledge it has never started back up again. One thing never truly answered was the question that nobody seemed to want to talk about. How did someone decide on the company to start this pilot program with? The bottom line is there is always someone watching, but the problem is not everyone is willing to tell. Could the real reason they were forthcoming be tied to the fact this County Commissioner had created an atmosphere of tell it all and we will fix it? There were a few unhappy folks who were riding the bus. "What is done in the dark must come to the light and if it survives in the light, it is probably alright." Stacy Lee George

The initial beginning of the bus story is of importance here. The citizen noticing something out of the ordinary and saying simply "Have a look." A very helpful thing to encourage that helping attitude was the comforting knowledge someone who does not put up with the abuse of power by those in authority would definitely "Have a look." No reason to not tell Stacy. This knowledge is not necessarily forthcoming if citizens do not trust someone to do the right thing. This whole issue was not illegal, but it was unfair to other groups of people who had a long commute to work as well.

Psalm 41:1

Blessed is the one who considers the poor! In the day of trouble the Lord delivers him

DECATUR DAILY

Sunday, June 27, 2004

MCATS out of bounds?

Daily Photo by John Godbey

An MCATS bus drops off passengers in Florette.

Morgan resident discovers system transporting workers to Gadsden

By Sheryl Marsh
Daily Staff Writer

James Cooper was curious when he tailed a Morgan County Area Transportation System bus into Gadsden.

The Morgan County resident's curiosity vanished when he saw a group of men get off a bus and head into the Goodyear Tire plant.

Cooper said he knew then that MCATS is going beyond local routes to provide transportation, a practice that he said is an injustice to local people who don't have transportation.

"One time I saw a group of senior citizens get off the bus at Jack's," Cooper said of the fast-food restaurant. "They went in and came out with ice cream. I said, 'This is a good thing; that's what it's all about.'"

Please see MCATS, page A8

MCATS

Continued from page A1

"But then when I observed a group of healthy men getting out of their parked cars and into the MCATS bus, I thought, 'This is wrong,'" he said.

It is legal for MCATS to provide a "van pool" service for any group to and from work, according to Director Debra Rains and an official with the state Department of Transportation.

"Other counties have been doing this for years and DOT used to question me about why we weren't doing it," Rains said.

Wiley Brooks, a transportation planner with DOT, supported Rains.

"The Federal Transit Administration and DOT encourage our providers to be involved in van pooling or work route activities," Brooks said.

"It may be legal, but it's not right," said Cooper. "Something ain't right when ... seniors don't have a way to get somewhere in this county. I observed the bus hauling a group of healthy young men and then drop them back off to their fancy four-wheel-drive trucks and super cabs."

Rains said she started the van pool 18 months ago, and issued a van and bus to two groups of eight men for transportation to work at the tire plant in Gadsden. Each man pays $30 per week, a fee that Rains said she set to cover maintenance and gasoline costs.

"I factored all that into what we're charging them," Rains said.

It appears, however, that MCATS is barely breaking even by charging $30 per week.

Combined, the workers pay $1,280 per month. The estimated fuel cost alone is $1,875 a month, based on the county's current price per gallon and the buses' average fuel mileage. That does not include maintenance, repairs and insurance.

Two of the workers drive the buses and each has a gas card. Rains said they received training and undergo drug testing like MCATS employees. She said she placed them on the agency's insurance plan.

The trips are putting an estimated 46,540 miles a year on each bus, according to calculations based on a round trip of 179 miles a day, five days a week.

Rains said, however, the workers are using older vehicles that are out of circulation from the regular fleet. She said she removes vehicles once they reach 100,000 miles on the odometer. She said it's more profitable to rent the older vehicles than sell them because they only get $300 and $400 for some they sold through Gov-Deals, a network to sell government items.

The tire plant workers use a 15-passenger van and a 15-passenger commuter bus.

Rains said she uses some of the money that the men pay to help match funds for grants for the federal/state-funded program. The county pays most of the matching funds.

> *'It may be legal, but it's not right. Something ain't right when ... seniors don't have a way to get somewhere in this county. I observed the bus hauling a group of healthy young men and then drop them back off to their fancy four-wheel-drive trucks and super cabs.'*
>
> — James Cooper, interested citizen

Chasing buses

Cooper said a newspaper editorial sparked his interest in the transportation program and followed the buses.

"The editorial talked about how poor transportation is in the state and this county," he said.

"For months, I saw these people ... and took down the bus numbers. They got in buses in the evening and the next morning they came back in the buses. They left their fancy cars parked at a grocery store in Florette and across from a store in Decatur, and somebody would then take the buses and park them in a parking lot across from the store," Cooper said.

He said he reported his findings to District 4 Commissioner Stacy George and asked him to check into the matter.

George said he talked with Rains about the issue and although the practice appears to be legal, he is concerned about it because she didn't bring it before the County Commission, and because the transportation service should focus mainly on local needs.

"If it's going to be used to subsidize income like I feel it's being used, we need to let all the people know about it and get them qualified according to income," George said. "We need to set some higher fees for people making higher salaries. For example, at Wayne's Farms where several people from my district work, there may be some people who would want to van pool to cut down on their travel expenses. I am continuing to look into the matter."

No commission approval

Brooks said the County Commission should approve any rates set for transportation services and MCATS should advertise such programs.

Rains said she does not recall getting the commission's approval.

"I know I wouldn't have done it without them saying it was OK, but I don't remember it being on the agenda," Rains said.

George said the matter has not been before the commission.

"Not unless it was in disguise with a grant or something. If we're supposed to approve it, we need to find out why it didn't come before us," he said.

Commission Chairman Larry Bensich, who is in charge of day-to-day operations, said he knew about the van pooling and approves of it.

"This is another part of the operation that they can utilize to help financially, and it's perfectly fine," Bensich said.

Rains said, although she promoted the transportation program publicly by speaking to various groups, she didn't advertise van pooling, but that does not mean it's not for everybody.

"We don't discriminate. It doesn't matter if a person has 18 cars in their driveway; if they want to ride a bus, we have to let them," she said.

She said anyone who has a group and wants to van pool to work may contact her about the service.

Currently the Gadsden van pool is the only one. Rains said no one else has approached her about it.

Cooper said he talked with Rains and he is still not satisfied.

"I know how these good ol' boys like to take care of their own and their system is still alive and well," he said. "They can car pool with each other. They don't need to be using MCATS. Those buses are for people who do not have a way to go shop, to the doctor or just to get some ice cream."

Tuesday, June 29, 2004

Commission meeting heated on long-distance MCATS trips

Stacy George
Commissioner

Larry Bensich
Chairman

George to Bensich: *"Mr. Chairman, I'm not going to end my questioning. I've got 16 more minutes, whether you listen to it or not."*

By Sheryl Marsh
Daily Staff Writer

A county commissioner questioned the Morgan County Area Transportation System director Monday about why she provides two vehicles to send workers to Gadsden while not promoting van pooling to local industries.

The questions led to a heated exchange between commissioners as District 4 Commissioner Stacy George sought information from MCATS Director Debra Rains.

THE DAILY reported Sunday that workers at a tire plant are driving two vehicles an estimated 179 miles roundtrip a day to Gadsden. Each of the 16 workers pays $30 a week. Now, George told Rains, he is receiving calls about the long-distance van pooling.

"Everybody wants a bus to transport workers. Obviously it's legal, but it's not right," George said of the trips outside the county. "Have you ever run notices in the newspaper to let people know you had van pooling?"

She answered no, but said she spoke to

Please see MCATS, page A7

MCATS

Continued from page A1

groups throughout the county about various services that MCATS offers.

Also, she said, North-central Alabama Regional Council of Governments had meetings in the past where they discussed van pooling, but only nine or 10 people attended.

She said she has never advertised van pooling specifically.

"Did you tell them they could pay $30 a week to ride a bus to their jobs? George asked.

"No," she answered.

"We need to have a public meeting about this," George said.

Then, Commission Chairman Larry Bensich intervened.

"The system is slowly growing," Bensich said. "We had nine, worn-out buses when it first started and now we have gone to a fleet of safe vehicles. We didn't have the equipment to do that van pool back then. If y'all start bickering about this, we're going to see another program go down."

As George started to ask Rains another question, Bensich said the questioning should cease and tried to go on to another agenda item.

"Mr. Chairman, I'm not going to end my questioning," George said. "I've got 16 more minutes, whether you listen to it or not.

"This is worse than giving somebody free trash service in another county," George added, in reference to past accusations that Morgan County provided free garbage service to a supervisor's sister in Marshall County.

George told Rains about a man who called him who has a mentally challenged relative who works for Terrell Industries.

"He makes only $27 every two weeks. They need a bus. Can they get one?" he asked Rains.

"If they can come up with eight people, I'll be glad to work with them," she said.

District 3 Commissioner Jeff Clark said he attended public meetings in another setting with NARCOG officials for a needs assessment of MCATS and few residents attended.

George told Rains he wants everybody in the county to know about the van pooling service.

"We want to let people know that anybody who wants a bus can get one for $30 a week. You'll have a big influx of people wanting buses," he said.

"You're about to make a decision on whether you're going to support residents in Morgan County or people who need buses to go outside of the county."

Rains said to advertise to everybody will force the commission to come up with more money for buses.

"You're going to have to come out of your pocket to help buy more buses when you do this," Rains said of publicizing the service.

The van pool to Gadsden is the only one in the county and Rains said the men contacted her about the buses.

George got a motion passed to have three public hearings July 13. The first meeting will be at 10 a.m. and the second at 1 p.m. in the commission meeting room of the courthouse. A third meeting will be at 6 p.m. at the county engineer's shop at 580 Shull Road in Hartselle.

"This is so people who work different shifts in the county can attend. We need to let all the residents know about this service," George said.

James Cooper, a county resident, complained to THE DAILY last week after he observed men using two MCATS vehicles to go to work every day at Gadsden's Goodyear Tire plant.

Rains said she uses some of the money from the van pool to help pay local matches for federal grants for the program, but calculations show that the county is barely covering its fuel cost.

Combined, the men pay $1,280 per month and fuel cost alone is $1,875 a month, based on the county's cost per gallon and the vehicles' average fuel mileage. The cost of maintenance, such as oil changes and tires, is not included in the amount.

The men have been using the buses for 18 months.

THE DECATUR DAILY

RIVERFRONT C1

Tuesday, July 13, 2004

County hears van pool complaints

Residents oppose MCATS providing transportation to Goodyear plant workers in Gadsden

By Sheryl Marsh
DAILY Staff Writer
smarsh@decaturdaily.com • 340-2437

Morgan County residents at a public hearing this morning were more interested in complaining about buses transporting workers out of town than asking for a ride.

Some of the employees of the Goodyear tire plant in Gadsden, who use a Morgan County Area Transportation System vehicle to van pool to work, were at the meeting and defended their right to the public service.

The County Commission held the first of three meetings set for today to allow residents to inquire about MCATS services.

Bob Conner of Decatur questioned who would be liable if one of the drivers wrecked a vehicle. County Attorney Bill Shinn said he was researching the issue, but could not give a solid answer. Shinn said tentatively that the county would not be liable, that it would depend on circumstances.

Conner asked MCATS Director Debra Rains whether the time conflicted with the time buses were to run regular routes to pick up people for local rides and she said it did not, because the workers use the buses from 7 p.m. to 7 a.m. She said her drivers start at 7 a.m. and the van pool cannot interfere with daily scheduling because the workers use vehicles that are out of circulation.

Rains denied that she was barely breaking even because the tire plant employees each pay $20 per week to ride the buses. There are two groups of eight and their total fees amounts to $1,280 a month. Estimated fuel cost for the vehicles alone, however, is $1,878 based on the buses' average fuel mileage.

James Cooper, the man who said he watched the workers for months going to Gadsden and back, said he still does not think the county should allow long-distance van pooling because local people need transportation within the county.

Please see MCATS, page C2

MCATS

Continued from page C1

"I didn't know I was going to start all this and cost all this damn money when I reported what I thought was illegal," Cooper said of the public hearing, where a paid court reporter took notes.

He said the day after people read about his complaint in THE DAILY three weeks ago, he started to get calls about not being able to get local rides with MCATS.

"A lot of people said they tried to get a ride and were turned down. It don't make sense to me," Cooper said. "It just struck me as unordinary that two-thirds of the people don't have a ride at any given time."

Donald Henry, one of the Goodyear employees, said the public meeting offended him and others. "This meeting seems to be a public lynching to us," Henry said.

He said they did nothing wrong and they asked about the service because they knew of another county transit system that provided buses for workers to the Dunlop tire plant, their former workplace in Huntsville.

Another Goodyear employee, Ricky Camp, said he saw Cooper following them and mentioned it to his co-workers. If Cooper had asked them, they would have told him what they were doing, he said.

Other workers spoke and praised MCATS for the service.

District 4 Commissioner Stacy George said the issue is that Rains failed to advertise van pooling so that others could use the service.

Other meetings were scheduled at 1 p.m. today at the courthouse and this evening at 6 at the county engineer's shop on Shull Road in Hartselle.

THE DECATUR DAILY, [illegible]

Bennich, George end meeting with heated exchange

By Sheryl Marsh
DAILY Staff Writer
smarsh@decaturdaily.com • 340-2437

The Morgan County Commission meeting today ended with Chairman Larry Bennich and District 4 Commissioner Stacy George arguing to the point of George asking if he should call the sheriff.

George had just finished apologizing to a group of workers who use county transportation to van pool to their job at Goodyear Tire in Gadsden. He apologized for saying weeks ago that the van pooling situation was worse than the county giving free garbage service across the county line.

Then, George said he was going to meet with officials at Terrell Industries to see if the county could

Please see Heat, page A7

Heat

Continued from page A1

help them with transportation for workers with handicaps.

That's when Bennich spoke.

"I wasn't going to say nothing, but since you brought it up, I heard about you calling Terrell Industries a sweatshop, Mr. George, but if you mean that up there's going to be some serious problems between me and you," said Bennich, who is not seeking re-election.

"Larry, you've accused me of playing politics with the microphone, but now that's exactly what you're doing with the microphone. Your days are numbered, Mr. Chairman ..."

"This meeting is adjourned," Bennich said.

Stacy George

As the commissioners disassembled, Bennich went to George and said, "If you mean that up, I'll get you and I don't care who knows it."

"Do I need to call the sheriff, Larry?" George said. "Do I need to call the sheriff?"

"I don't care who you call," Bennich answered.

After the meeting George said he did not call Terrell Industries a sweatshop.

"I support Terrell Industries," George said. "The only reason I'm going to meet with them is to see if we can't get them a bus because I've had people call me about their current situation,

Larry Bennich

riding MCATS, paying $4 a day like the Gadsden pool. So if we can get them a bus, they wouldn't be paying but $1 a day if it's figured on the same formula they use for the other van pool."

Bennich said his interest in Terrell Industries is the fact that his daughter works there.

"We've worked hard to have a place for my daughter and other people's children to have a place to work," Bennich said. "He (George) has a way of destroying things and he needs to stay away from Terrell Industries. It's certainly not a sweatshop. I heard that's what he called it from two good sources."

Bennich, George square off at end of commission meet

By Sheryl Marsh
DAILY Staff Writer
smarsh@decaturdaily.com • 340-2437

▶ Related stories, C2

Morgan County Commission Chairman Larry Bennich abruptly ended a meeting Monday during an argument between him and Commissioner Stacy George, and George asked if he should call the sheriff.

George had just finished apologizing to a group of workers who use county transportation to van-pool to their job at Goodyear Tire in Gadsden. The District 4 commissioner apologized for saying weeks ago that the van pooling situation was worse than the county giving free garbage

Please see Words, page A8

Larry Bennich

Stacy George

THE DECATUR DAILY, Tuesday, July 27, 2004

Words

Continued from page A1

service across the county line.

Then, George said he was going to meet with officials at Terrell Industries to see if the county could help them with transportation for workers with handicaps.

That's when Bennich spoke.

"I wasn't going to say nothing, but since you brought it up, I heard about you calling Terrell Industries a sweatshop, Mr. George, but if you mean that up there's going to be some serious problems between me and you," said Bennich, who is not seeking re-election.

"Larry, you've accused me of playing politics with the microphone, but now that's exactly what you're doing with the microphone. Your days are numbered, Mr. Chairman ..."

"This meeting is adjourned," Bennich said.

As the commissioners disassembled, Bennich went to George and said, "If you mean that up, I'll get you and I don't care who knows it."

"Do I need to call the sheriff, Larry?" George said. "Do I need to call the sheriff?"

"I don't care who you call," Bennich answered.

After the meeting George said he did not call Terrell Industries a sweatshop.

"I support Terrell Industries," George said. "The only reason I'm going to meet with them is to see if we can't get them a bus because I've had people call me about their current situation, riding MCATS, paying $4 a day like the Gadsden pool. So if we can get them a bus, they wouldn't be paying but $1 a day if it's figured on the same formula they use for the other van pool."

Bennich said his interest in Terrell Industries is the fact that his daughter works there.

"We've worked hard to have a place for my daughter and other people's children to have a place to work," Bennich said. "He (George) has a way of destroying things and he needs to stay away from Terrell Industries. It's certainly not a sweatshop. I heard that's what he called it from two good sources."

DECATUR

"Our country ... may she always be in the right; but our country, right or wrong." — *Unknown*

Wednesday, July 14, 2004

Jean Callahan of Hartselle told local and state officials that she doesn't think it's fair for her brother-in-law to pay the same price to ride an MCATS bus locally as those who van-pool to Gadsden.

DAILY Photo by Emily Saunders

Residents complain bus service unfair

MCATS Director Debra Perra answered questions of Morgan residents who questioned about a van-pooling service and offered, but did not advertise.

By Sheryl Marsh
DAILY Staff Writer
sheryl.marsh@decaturdaily.com • 340-2437

Jean Callahan said she doesn't understand why a Morgan County Area Transportation System bus doesn't charge her brother-in-law a ride for her severely challenged brother-in-law to go to the doctor.

Another does she understand why he has to pay $4 a day to ride the bus, the same fee that employees pay to go 115 miles a day commuting to the Goodyear Tire plant in Gadsden.

"He shouldn't have to pay that to go to the doctor," Callahan said.

Callahan was speaking at one of three meetings that the County Commission had Tuesday in which public input on the transportation service. The service came under fire recently for providing free rides to local employees in Decatur.

Most residents complained about the Gadsden trips rather than asking for van-pooling service to local industries.

MCATS Director Debra Perra said the special health center does not subsidize pay for, claims

Bus
Continued from page A1

to ride the buses and that's why Callahan's brother-in-law has to pay the full fare.

"All he rides is from Parkinsonwood Road to Flint and he still has to pay the same as those going to Gadsden," Callahan said. "That's not right. He shouldn't have to pay that kind of money. He does not have it."

Callahan and about 36 other Hartselle residents questioned state and local officials during the last public hearing. They said they want the system to be more accommodating for local transportation needs.

Oscar Waugh said he calls for rides but does not get one every time.

"Sometimes they don't come by and just ride," Waugh said.

Perra said she would check into the matter.

Charles Kirby of Decatur said he thought the transit system was for local people who need transportation, and it doesn't seem right for people who claim federal subsidies to be able to earn the system be a corporate van-pooling.

"I'm concerned about what's the most efficient use and the lowest use of taxpayers' money," Kirby said.

Jim Nix, a transit transportation planner with the state Department of Transportation, who sent the meeting, said that a system should provide transportation for anyone who wants to ride.

He said van-pooling allows more riders to go out of the county and state. Nix said DOT developed a formula to calculate

what riders pay for van-pooling.

He said uses of the buses in rural medical neighborhoods, work and recreation.

Lori Cooper of Somerville said it's not right and residents should appeal to federal officials to get it changed.

Charles Brasel asked if he could get a bus to take a group of eight to Smyrna.

Nix answered yes.

"Why not?" Brasel asked, "So said they could be used for recreation."

Nix said special groups such as senior citizens, mental health agencies and welfare agencies could employ the buses in any recreational trips.

James Gregg, a Somerville resident who followed MCATS issues in the Gadsden plant and reported the trips to THE DAILY said he had been writing about the issue for months.

"We're doing MCATS service with THE DAILY that the agency isn't violating, get access to various van-pools, Brasel said he's appeared the service was barely leaving, even as he's changing the Gadsden workers for a day. That does not because van-discovery and interstate cost.

In Tuesday meeting, Brasel said the transportation van offers average about 14 miles per gallon.

David Callahan, president of ModAction, said the agency's per vehicles had its taxes only average eight miles per gallon. He said he's never seen how MCATS saved by making money because of the fuel cost.

Nix said he realizes the service has problems and the state

has a commission that has advised cities advising a portion of the service work with state, he said helped back chartering getting for the county buses the economic could lower cost of the plant with MCATS.

District 4 Commissioner Stacy Georgy complained that Perra should have advertised the van-pooling service so that all interested could know.

Perra said she didn't advertise because it doesn't save enough for MCATS.

Speaking at a meeting in Decatur, David Henry, one of the Goodyear employees, said the public hearings attended were not others.

"The carding seems to be a public meeting for us," Henry said.

He said they did nothing wrong and blew asked about the service because they have of a van-pool from another public transit station for workers in the Decatur tire plant, they former worker said.

Commissioner Stacey Ferry from Swan Shoemock, who spoke over the public hearings said she was interested in making sure they worked as well as they clear that on the van-pool.

"They found a ride," Shoemock said, "and they took it."

MAINTENANCE DIRECTOR, "YOU MEAN I CAN'T NEVER DRINK A BEER"

Each year the Morgan County Commission has budget hearings dealing with all county courthouse departments including everything except the state court system functions. I remember this budget very well. We ask all department heads and elected officials to trim their budgets by about 15 percent. With a new 23-million-dollar jail to pay for we felt there needed to be a decrease in excess spending.

Everyone was doing great until the Maintenance Department Head showed up. He arrogantly stated there was nothing to cut. While looking over his budget I noticed something called on-call pay. This amount was 11,804 dollars per year. I ask simply," what is this on-call pay?" He explained that the courthouse was built on top of an underground spring and the sump pumps must continuously run to keep the water level from flooding the courthouse. That all sounded good, but what came next left the room in silence. I stated, "so this is really overtime money in the event you are called in for emergency purposes". Basically, "this is the money you pay people so they can sit at home and drink a beer if they want to." I immediately said, "**The Morgan County Commission should not be in the business of paying people to stay sober.**" Next, I recommended he rotate this on call position around. This money should only be used if there is a need when someone is called in to fix an urgent problem. The commission then recommended he trim his budget and come back to the commission. He came back deciding he would eliminate one of his employees, but the on-call pay would stay in his budget the way it originally was. At this point, I recommended we could easily cut his budget by simply eliminating the Maintenance Director's position. The "end" result at my recommendation is the county commission did just that and the courthouse maintenance did not miss a beat. You see in government if no one is watching and asking questions this abuse of funds simply happens. Misuse of money is going on at the county, city, state, and federal level right now. The only thing needed in accountability is someone not in the political click to call it out and reporters to report it. If the taxpayers know the facts, they will demand it to be stopped.

What can be learned about abuse of power from the Maintenance Director? There was intent, incentive, and opportunity. There was a lack of either knowledge or interest to stop this conduct by those able to see it.

First, in dealing with corruption a question must be asked, "Where does this money go?" That is often a good question. If the answer is vague get the clear facts even if you are led through whatever is occurring in small beginning steps. You see there are no dumb questions in life, as a matter of fact, there are only dumb answers.

Many times, at this point a Eureka moment can come into play if one looks at what actions are taking place as if one is seeing it for the first time.

The last step is acting on ending the corruption and implementing the new plan. It requires what I call "gumption". This is the initiative to stop the corruption and put a firewall in place to stop it from spreading.

When you first ask the question – "Why is the money being spent?" A good clearing of the throat and a shaking of the head side to side when something seems fishy could mean gumption is about to come on strong.

Hebrews 13:5

Make sure that your character is free from the love of money, being content with what you have; for He Himself has said, "I will never desert you, nor will I ever forsake you,"

Fire maintenance head to cut costs?

THE DECATUR DAILY
RIVERFRONT
Tuesday, July 26, 2005

By Sheryl Marsh
DAILY Staff Writer
smarsh@decaturdaily.com • 340-2437

A Morgan County department head suggested laying off employees to lower his 2006 budget, but a commissioner recommended firing him instead.

District 4 Commissioner Stacy George and Personnel Director Jack Underwood plan to meet with the county attorney today to discuss Maintenance Director Dwight Gardner's employment.

Gardner went before the commission Monday for a budget hearing and had neglected to include crucial maintenance supplies like cleaning chemicals.

The commission has proposed that each department cut its budget by 15 percent, and Gardner said the only way he could get down to about $1.08 million from $1.38 million was to eliminate multiple line items.

He also said he had another budget prepared that was higher than the one he submitted. He said the real solution is to lay off employees.

The commission reviewed his budget and had him fill in the empty blanks verbally. At the end, his budget was $80,000 over.

Gardner's annual salary, plus benefits, is $69,828, and after he left the room, George made a suggestion.

"I know exactly what we can do. We can fire the maintenance director and let the other people keep their jobs. His salary and benefits would put it just about where it needs to be," said George. "There's a leak in this building right now that needs fixing, and the air is always out of order. We need to do something."

Commissioner Richard Lyons favored the suggestion as well.

Chairman John Glasscock recommended the meeting with the county attorney to discuss the matter.

Although Gardner left many line items blank, he put down $11,804 for on-call pay for employees and himself.

All the commissioners balked at that and questioned him about it. Gardner said he gets on-call pay as well. They quickly removed that amount from his budget.

Please see Costs, page C2

Costs

Continued from page C1

As maintenance director, Gardner supervises 16 employees, including the courthouse receptionist. The employees' pay ranges from $7 per hour to $16 per hour. Longtime employees, with more than 20 years, get the higher pay.

Gardner has been the maintenance director 15 years and his hourly wage is $24.

Juvenile budget

In a separate meeting with juvenile officials, the commission learned that the county might lose four of its five beds at a juvenile detention center in Tuscumbia.

Chief Juvenile Probation Officer Harry Williams said he cut other line items before decreasing housing funding from $162,400 for five beds to $30,428, which will pay for one bed.

After the meeting, the commission worked with Williams' budget and got it down to $30,000 over the projected 2006 budget, which had a 15 percent cut.

In doing so, the commission brought the number of beds to three.

Budget hearings continue today.

Morgan County commissioners quiet about fate of maintenance director

By Sheryl Marsh
DAILY Staff Writer
smarsh@decaturdaily.com • 340-2437

Morgan County commissioners had a lot to say Monday when talking about possibly firing the courthouse maintenance director, but Tuesday after a conference with the county attorney nobody is saying anything.

Commissioners were angered Monday when Maintenance Director Dwight Gardner presented an incomplete budget and recommended laying off some of his employees. After meeting with him, Commissioner Stacy George suggested his termination. Commissioner Richard Lyons agreed with the suggestion.

Gardner met with the commission Monday for a budget hearing and he said a layoff in his department would be the solution to balancing his budget.

In making his recommendation, George said Gardner's salary and benefits of $69,828 would put the budget about where it should be.

George and the county's personnel director met with Attorney Bill Shinn on Tuesday to discuss the issue.

Lyons did not attend the meeting.

"At this time, I don't have a comment on anything personal as far as he (Gardner) is concerned," George

Please see Morgan, page B2

B2

Morgan

Continued from page B1

said. "But I am going to pursue the same direction I started. We're in the process of budget cuts, and we're trying to cut costs and that's my whole goal. My philosophy is to combine agencies to save money."

Lyons said, "At this time I don't have a comment, until we get things finalized."

Gardner declined comment on the matter Tuesday.

The commission told department heads to lower budgets by 15 percent. Gardner told commissioners the only way he could meet that request was to eliminate multiple line items, including things like cleaning supplies. He then told the commission that layoffs would be necessary to balance the budget.

Gardner has been the county's maintenance director for 15 years and he supervises 16 maintenance and janitorial employees.

THE DECATUR DAILY, Thursday, July 28, 2005

Maintenance director: I've done my best

By Sheryl Marsh
DAILY Staff Writer

Morgan County Maintenance Director Dwight Gardner told the County Commission that he designed the meeting room where commissioners discussed firing him and that, over the years, he's saved the county lots of money.

After giving commissioners a verbal profile of himself and his 15-year county employment, Gardner challenged them to go through with the firing.

Gardner, who has a degree from Athens State University, began his speech Wednesday by telling the commission that he is a U.S. Marine veteran.

"I've been here when this county didn't have much money and I'm here again when the county does not have much money," said Gardner. "This room you're in was nothing, and I designed the space with the help of the chairman at that time."

Former Chairman Larry Bennich hired Gardner.

"I manage my people to the best of my ability and we save this county more money than any other department," he said.

> "I've done the best I can do, and if you want to fire me, then so be it. There are other jobs."
>
> Dwight Gardner, Maintenance director

Commissioner Stacy George suggested terminating Gardner after Gardner said the solution to balancing his budget was laying off some of his staff. Commissioner Richard Lyons agreed with George.

Gardner said Thursday he does not have the authority to approve layoffs because the personnel manual states that the commission has that power. He said he was not in favor of laying off employees.

The commission directed all department heads to cut their budgets 15 percent. The budget Gardner presented Monday eliminated key line items like cleaning supplies, so that he could comply with the directive.

"I have done the best I can do, and if you want to fire me, then so be it. There are other jobs," Gardner said.

After he finished, he asked if commissioners had questions. There was silence, even after Gardner left the room.

Commissioners continue to keep quiet about their next move.

August 9, 2005

Maintenance budget fight in 4th round

Morgan's new figures cut 3 workers, add on-call pay

By Sheryl Marsh
DAILY Staff Writer
smarsh@decaturdaily.com • 340-2437

The embattled maintenance director at the Morgan County Courthouse presented a revised budget Monday, which removed three people from his payroll and added on-call pay to salaries for five workers, including himself.

On-call pay became a punching bag for District 4 County Commissioner Stacy George, who wants to eliminate Dwight Gardner's position as maintenance director.

"You mean to tell me you came in here a third time, wanting to get rid of employees and give yourself and others a pay raise?" George said.

"It's not a pay raise. They've been getting this every year," Gardner said.

He said former Commission Chairman Larry Bennich approved the on-call pay, which the director before him received as well.

Although only one employee is on call each week, the others and Gardner still get the pay even when it's not their turn to be on call.

> "You mean to tell me I can't never drink a beer?"
>
> Dwight Gardner, Morgan County Courthouse maintenance director

Gardner said he was told last year to convert the on-call allotment of $130 per month for five people to salary, but that did not go through.

"Well, today that's a fringe benefit, and it is not going to be paid anymore," George said. "We're not going to pay people to sit home and eat Moon Pies and potato chips and watch TV. As maintenance director you're always on call anyway."

"You mean to tell me I can't never drink a beer?" Gardner asked.

"I'm saying you need to make sure someone is available to handle maintenance, if you're not around," answered George.

Gardner said he added 94 cents per hour to his and the

Please see Budget, page C2

THE DECATUR DAILY, Thursday, September 1, 2005

Ex-maintenance director: politics behind dismissal

By Sheryl Marsh
DAILY Staff Writer
smarsh@decaturdaily.com • 340-2437

The former director of the Morgan County Maintenance Department told the personnel board Wednesday that commissioners fired him for political reasons, not to save money.

District 1 Commissioner Jeff Clark backed ex-Maintenance Director Dwight Gardner's theory during a hearing before the personnel board.

The commission voted 3-1 to eliminate Gardner's post and terminate his employment Aug. 19. The resolution to fire Gardner stated that the action was for budgetary purposes, not because of job performance. Gardner, 47, appealed to the board.

"This is all because of political reasons and proving it is going to be difficult," Gardner said Wednesday during his hearing. "It has nothing to do with job performance and nothing to do with money. It's to do with me and it's personal."

Gardner represented himself and called witnesses, including all the commissioners.

County attorney Bill Shinn had Chairman John Glasscock testify about the budget process. Glasscock explained how he and employees in his office figured a proposed 2006 budget.

Please see Gardner, page B2

Gardner

Continued from page B1

He told how they arrived at asking for a 15 percent cut from each department.

Glasscock said Gardner's termination was strictly because of the budget and not for job performance or disciplinary reasons.

Gardner accused Commissioner Richard Lyons of plotting his firing with Glasscock and Commissioner Stacy George.

"You wouldn't admit that Mr. George, you and Mr. Glasscock set up the budget figures to take me down?" Gardner asked.

"Heck no," Lyons answered.

Gardner asked Commissioner Kevin Murphy if he discussed his firing with anyone before the vote and he said he did not.

George, who was the first commissioner to recommend eliminating Gardner, told him that he was glad they had the votes to get rid of his job. He said it was to save money.

Commissioner Clark, who voted against firing Gardner, said when George first suggested firing Gardner, Lyons agreed. He said they talked about his job performance and that was the reason they wanted to fire him. In the last discussion, however, Clark said the commissioners' reason was due to the budget.

He told the board that Gardner should have his job back because the county needs his expertise, especially with the new jail.

Human Resources Director Jack Underwood said the commission did not follow the personnel manual in terminating Gardner.

One of the board members pointed out that the manual states that the commission is the ultimate authority on employment.

Gardner told board members that he would like for them to recommend reinstatement to his job.

He said the commissioners dislike him because he supported former commissioners, who were Democrats.

Shinn urged the board to uphold Gardner's firing.

Chairman Lawrence Brown said the board will give its decision to Glasscock.

In the meantime, Gardner is on administrative leave with pay and the maintenance operation is under supervision of the Engineering Department.

Budget

Continued from page C1

employees' salaries. During his first budget hearing in July, he had allotted $11,000 for on-call pay in a separate line item.

When presenting his revised budget Monday, Gardner recommended laying off two employees and moving the switchboard operator to the County Commission's payroll.

Gardner said the switchboard operator used to be under the commission and the job is the least critical to his maintenance operation.

One of the employees he suggested laying off is still on probation and the other employees are low in seniority.

Commissioner Jeff Clark asked if the operator's post would be needed after the county gets an automated phone system.

George and Commissioner Kevin Murphy were against eliminating the operator.

Clark said that was the purpose of getting the new system, but the other two commissioners said that was not their understanding. They said it was to save money by reducing the number of telephone lines.

Gardner offered another plan to remove a 22-year employee from his staff who handles mail and courier duties for the courthouse.

"You're still saying you've got to do away with personnel, and you're still holding your position. Is that not greedy?" George asked.

Gardner said he doesn't want to lay off anyone, but that's the only way he can lower his budget by the commission-ordered 15 percent.

He said if the operator and the courier left his payroll, that would save the county $83,454.

Commissioners told him that moving employees elsewhere would not save money.

Later, after two other budget hearings, Clark recommended eliminating the courthouse operator's post after the new phone system is working.

George said people like to talk with someone when they call the courthouse.

Operator vs. automated

County Administrator Willa Dockery said the operator helps callers who don't know which court office they need. Also, she said, about 600 calls go through the switchboard daily.

Clark said the on-call pay should remain in Gardner and his employees' salaries.

"You'd be taking away these people's grocery money," Clark said.

"You learn to live with what you make," Murphy said.

District 2 Commissioner Richard Lyons, who said earlier that Gardner was not doing his job, said no one has even reprimanded Gardner. Lyons also said that should be up to the chairman.

George referred to the county's personnel manual, which states that the commission is the appointing authority for department heads.

The commission plans to revisit Gardner's situation after all budget hearings end.

RACY EMAILS TO PORN (THE REAL ISSUE WAS ACCESS TO PUBLIC RECORDS)

A racy email exchange started the investigation, but desperation and bare-knuckle politics stopped it. There are only two questions that sum this email scandal up. Question number one is: "How far will I go to retrieve public records in the form of emails?" Question number two is: "How far will courthouse politicians go to stop me from getting public records?"

I remember this scandal well and it started at the end of the November 2006 election cycle. The email hack came from the main server in the Morgan County Courthouse. The email leak was done with the intention to destroy two county commissioners including the chairman of the county commission and another unnamed commissioner. Little did the hacker know exactly what the Chairman Pro Tem, who happened to be me, was about to uncover. Who in the Morgan County Courthouse really had something to hide? This is how it all started to unfold; our Human Resource Director in the courthouse emailed the Chairman of the County Commission a racy email. Next, the chairman emailed the racy email to the Mayor of Decatur. The leaked email first made its scene to the public by an investigative reporter at WHNT 19 in Huntsville, Alabama. After the discovery the Morgan County Human Resource Director was fired quickly. I happened to be the Chairman Pro Tem of the county commission at the time this scandal started.

The Chairman of the Commission chose to recuse himself of the situation leaving me to lead the investigation. I immediately ordered seizure of all county computer hard drives turning mine in first. All elected officials ultimately participated either by hard drive or email server except for the Revenue Commissioner as well as the Sheriff. I knew time was of essence and things would be deleted and destroyed quickly from the hard drives. The Revenue Commissioner changed the locks on the doors to the Revenue Office and locked two of the department's hard drives in a locked safe including her own hard drive. I knew at that point there was something to hide. At the same time, I decided we need to go to the main server and copy the emails to a disk for review. The Sheriff immediately told me point blank; "if you leave with that disk of the main server emails you will be arrested". He stated that the Sheriff's department emails on the main server had NCIC information, Homeland Security Information, and on-going investigations that could only be viewed by law enforcement. I stated we have an APOST certified Law Enforcement Officer doing the forensic computer investigation. I had already recommended and passed a resolution hiring a computer forensic expert law enforcement officer out of Jefferson County. This would take some of the politics out of the mix. I made the decision not to leave with the disk after consulting several attorneys advising me I would be arrested if I left the computer room with the disk. I decided the copied disk of the main server should be put in a safe and left in the computer department of the courthouse. I also purchased some surveillance cameras for security of the safe.

At this point we had all the courthouse computers run through forensics and we found pornographic movies on the Chairman's computer. The situation changed from racy emails to full blown porn. It was time someone asked the Commission Chairman to resign for the betterment of Morgan County. The Chairman stated he would not be leaving. The only two elected officials not working with the investigation were the Revenue Commissioner and the Sheriff. I called a special meeting of the county commission to pass a resolution taking court action to get the main server disk for forensic investigation. My resolution failed, and commission members folded. The commission basically folded leaving the investigation to be completed with a report from our forensic specialist on the hard drives we retrieved. I had only one choice left and that was to take court action myself. I obtained a lawyer at my expense and a circuit Judge was assigned to the case. In my lawsuit I filed court action to obtain the main server disk I secured in the safe. The court action named our IT Director, Commission Chairman, and the new Chairman Pro Tem District One Commissioner in the lawsuit and the Judge required a monetary deposit of 4500 dollars to hold a restraining order on the public records. I raised the money to secure the records and the Judge then issued a temporary restraining order protecting the public records. The Judge ultimately ruled the elected officials would make available the emails that they feel are suitable for review with a third party being present. The third party would likely be a retired Judge that would be paid according to the amount of time required to review thousands of emails.

The "end" result was really a question. Is an email a public record? The answer is yes, but in Alabama we must clarify the term public record to include a precise description of emails on taxpayer paid for computers and main servers. The moral to this story is very simple. The Sheriff and the Revenue Commissioner went to great lengths to keep the public from access to computer hard drives and an email server. One important issue to note is that all elected officials paid by county taxpayer funds had no objections and the forensic computer expert found the computers to be clean except for the Sheriff and the Revenue Commissioner. In conclusion, the right of the public to see a public record is in jeopardy and the larger issue is without access to public records accountability is zero in government.

It cannot stress enough the importance of "The Alabama Open Records Law". The ability to see what has happened is a must. How it was done, who sent it and who received it always keeps what occurred in the light. The best deterrent of corruption is public awareness, and therefore we must always demand access to public records.

It should be noted that those with the power to hand over the information may not be aware of the law. It may also be possible the politicians have given strict orders to refuse access to public records. There should be a penalty so severe dealing with access to public records that the penalty would put the fear of GOD in people holding the key to the access of public records. It would be helpful if the custodian of information, a municipal clerk, a county clerk, etc. including their staff attend a class given by their superiors with this knowledge including materials to read as well as a test to pass.

There should also be a simpler remedy than a judge ordering the information which is public to be handed over. Of course, the open records laws I am speaking of are those of the federal government as well as state sunshine laws.

Exodus 23:2

You must not follow a crowd in wrongdoing. Do not testify in a lawsuit and go along with a crowd to pervert justice.

The Decatur Daily

50 CENTS
TUESDAY
JANUARY 9, 2007

THE INDEPENDENT VOICE OF THE TENNESSEE VALLEY SINCE 1912

Probe yields more racy photos

By Sheryl Marsh
[illegible]@decaturdaily.com
340-2437

"I regret using county computers for personal use and certainly it is not going to happen again."

Chairman John Glasscock
Who apparently had 30 inappropriate e-mails on his computer's hard drive

Morgan County Commission Chairman John Glasscock apologized Monday for sending sexually charged e-mails and said he will never make that mistake again.

Glasscock was reacting to a report from Wade Morgan of Alabama Forensic Data Services Inc., which found photographs of nude women on his computer as part of a County Commission probe into inappropriate use of county computers.

Morgan states in a written report that Glasscock's computer contained 30 inappropriate e-mails and former Human Resources Director Jack Underwood's had 96. Morgan said he based an violation of the county's personnel manual on the computers of 11 other elected officials, department heads and political appointees.

"I regret using county computers for personal use and certainly it is not going to happen again," Glasscock said. "None were sent to the courthouse, just to old buddies I worked with during the years."

Morgan said he found "pornographic images" on both men's computers and defined pornography, within the scope of his investigation, as "any image that shows a female's breast or the genitalia of a male or female."

That by itself is not a definition of pornography that would hold up in court.

A PowerPoint file, under Glasscock's name on the disc made as part of the report, contained 40 explicit pin-up type poses of nude women. The PowerPoint package was titled "Hot points … A Special Presentation."

The report contained 10 other e-mails under Glasscock's name. Probably the most offensive was a female on her knees performing oral sex on a police officer. The caption underneath read: "How to get out of a ticket."

Others were in the vein of a group of nude women piled into a mesh hammock on a beach setting or an image showing the buttocks of nude women pedaling bicycles in a race.

Images attributed to Underwood's computer were more graphic.

An image from Underwood to

Please see E-mail, page A4

E-mail

From page A1

Glasscock, which someone released to a WHNT-TV 19 reporter, resulted in the probe. The commission voted unanimously to look at the computer hard drives of all county officials, department heads and political appointees. The commission, however, reversed itself Dec. 28.

The result was the exclusion of the hard drives of Sheriff Greg Bartlett, Revenue Commissioner Amanda Scott and their employees. Both officials, citing sensitive material, blocked access. Board of Registrars Chairwoman Arlena Bailey and Probate Judge Bobby Day also cited sensitive information in their letters denying access.

Scott said she didn't want Morgan copying her hard drive and taking it to Birmingham.

Morgan, who is based in Homewood, said he had to copy the hard drives to filter information on his equipment.

Bartlett wrote a letter stating that Morgan was not to even look at his or his employees' e-mails on the main server.

In his report, Morgan said he was denied access to the county's main server because Bartlett objected.

Probe should continue?

District 4 Commissioner Stacy George said Morgan's findings indicate the investigation should continue and include Bartlett and Scott.

"We've done a little over half of the investigation, but it needs to be done right," said George. "Mr. Morgan's findings of pornographic material on two hard drives is evidence that the investigation needs to carry on. We need to look at them all, the sheriff and Ms. Scott's."

George, who headed the investigation as chairman pro tem, received the report from Morgan on Monday. He said he delivered copies of it to Commissioners Jeff Clark, Ken Livingston, Kevin Murphy and Glasscock.

The *Daily* gave George a written request, and he released the public record.

Clark is expected to be elected chairman pro tem Tuesday.

Morgan said his investigation included checking each computer for evidence of tampering with the hard disc drive or for the use of a data wiping program. He found none.

The forensics computer expert's report stated that Glasscock was the only one to send e-mails.

The County Commission, however, fired Underwood over an e-mail that showed nude women. He forwarded that a year ago to Glasscock, who sent it to a Decatur city official.

Not a crime

A federal prosecutor and the Morgan district attorney said sending adult material electronically to adults is not a crime.

Last month, George asked Glasscock to resign. Glasscock did not respond.

The commission meets Tuesday at 8:30 a.m.

Results of e-mail probe

These Morgan County elected officials, political appointees and department heads did not have sexually charged e-mails on county computer hard drives:

- License Commissioner Sue Baker Roan
- Deputy License Commissioner Patsy Dougherty
- District 1 Commissioner Jeff Clark
- District 2 Commissioner Ken Livingston
- District 3 Commissioner Kevin Murphy
- District 4 Commissioner Stacy George
- County Administrator Sybil Atkins
- Deputy Administrator, Carol Long
- Bruce Lackey, recreation director
- Debra Rains, transportation director
- John Allison, architect
- Greg Bodley, engineer
- Ed Sims, sales tax director
- David Hannah, data processing
- Claudia Roy, animal control director
- Ricky Brooks, garbage director
- Eddie Hicks, emergency management director

Saturday, Jan. 20, 2007

George sues commission, employees over e-mails

By CHARLES WHISENANT
The Arab Tribune

Morgan County Commissioner Stacy George has filed a petition in circuit court against all elected officials and employees of Morgan County. He is asking a judge to issue an order allowing him access to all public records, including e-mails on county computers.

George is paying for the petition out of his own pocket.

"I have retained an attorney personally, and I have personally paid a $232 filing fee," he says in a press release. "There will be no cost to the taxpayers of Morgan County."

While George, who is from Ryan, is suing all county employees, he specifically identifies Commission Chairman John Glasscock, commissioner Jeff Clark and data processing manager David Hannah as defendants.

"These are the people who blocked me from the county's computer server," George says. "The petition is against anyone who would try to stop me from accessing public records."

The issue stems from a recent investigation into misuse of the county's computers and e-mail system. Glasscock and a former employee had sent sexually explicit e-mails to each other that depicted naked women and pornographic-related topics.

The county's human resources director was fired late last year for his role in the scandal.

After the e-mail issue was made public, the commission authorized George to investigate the matter. However, on Dec. 28, the commission voted to end the investigation.

George wants the investigation continued.

"There is reason to believe that certain public officials and

Please see GEORGE, Page 3

George

Continued from Page 1

employees are abusing the use of county resources by engaging in e-mails of a pornographic nature, running personal businesses from county computers, keeping track of personal assets on county computers as well as other types of abuse of county resources," George says in his petition. "Such abuse may result in reimbursement to the county general fund for personal use of taxpayer resources, ethics complaints and/or criminal charges."

George also says that while micromanagement of county resources is not desirable on a daily basis, he feels it is necessary now.

"When an emergency arises, it is in order," he says.

Irreparable harm could result from the lack of access to public information, George says in the petition.

"Specifically, the law governing access has been broken," he says. "In addition, there is reason to believe that public material will be destroyed and lost forever."

The lawsuit was filed Wednesday. No hearings had been set on the matter as of Friday.

The Decatur Daily
SUNDAY, JANUARY 7, 2007

Opinion

EDITORIALS

Courthouse e-mail probe finished, but lacks sense of closure

A good salesman is a person who can successfully close the deal. A good public crusader is one who isn't constantly tilting at windmills.

Always tilting and rarely closing might well describe Morgan County Commissioner Stacy George who raises a multitude of seemingly legitimate questions about operation of county government but finds it difficult to bring closure.

The e-mail scandal at the courthouse is his latest failure. It started with someone other than Mr. George leaking to a television reporter a highly questionable e-mail sent from fired county human resources director Jack Underwood to Commission Chairman John Glasscock, who forwarded it to Decatur Mayor Don Kyle. Mayor Kyle said he requested that the chairman not send any more material of that nature.

Mr. George seized the occasion as an opportunity to purge the county's e-mail system of non-government-related transmissions because of an earlier charge that employees used their computers to participate in a chatroom site during work hours.

As chairman pro tem of the commission at the time of the e-mail investigation, Mr. George engineered the hiring of a Huntsville law firm to help with the case and to hire a computer expert to retrieve information from county-owned hard drives.

Morgan County Revenue Commissioner Amanda Scott and Sheriff Greg Bartlett refused to give up county-owned hard drives even though many county residents want to know what's on them. And because it's county equipment, people have a right to know.

Ms. Scott took her defiance a step further and changed the locks to her office at the courthouse. Mr. George said he tried to get something done about it, but Chairman Glasscock remains in charge of the courthouse.

Instead of granting Mr. George's request to have the locks changed back, Mr. Glasscock sent the other three commissioners a memorandum basically condoning the lock change by saying Ms. Scott would pay for the new locks out her discretionary fund. But that's taxpayers' money.

Glasscock knows that's not her personal money.

After obtaining a few hard drives without resistance, county commissioners voted to shut down the investigation.

Last week, a majority of the commissioners said they have been even handed in the matter — going ahead with inspecting the hard drives of the few people who willingly complied and closing the door on those who didn't.

Mr. George is a modern-day Don Quixote who happens to be part of a county government that foments intrigue.

Does that mean he is wrong?

Volume 74, No. 1 Thursday, January 4, 2007

Email investigation over

Call for chairman's resignation ignored

Cliff Knight
Hartselle Enquirer

A probe into the alleged illegal use of county-owned computers ended last week when the Morgan County Commission refused to go any further in its efforts to retrieve information on hard drives in the offices of Sheriff Greg Bartlett, Revenue Commissioner Amanda Scott and Probate Judge Bobby Day. Instead, they voted three to one to proceed with the processing of information they currently have in their possession and to follow up by making revisions needed to clarify and strengthen the existing computer use policy. District 4 Commissioner Stacy George cast the "no" vote.

Following a 30-minute executive session, George attempted without success to get the governing body to authorize legal action to retrieve the hard drives so that the investigation could be completed. He made a motion to that effect but it died for the lack of a second.

George said Wade Morgan of Alabama Forensic Data Services was able to collect information from about 80 percent of the hard drives in the courthouse before access was denied by Bartlett, Scott and Day. They all indicated that their hard drives contain sensitive information for which they are accountable to protect under the law.

"As things now stand, we can't function as a county government that is accountable to the people," George said. "That being the case, I think it's appropriate for me to ask Mr. Glasscock, our chairman, to resign."

See EMAIL, A5

Glasscock did not respond.

District 2 Commissioner Ken Livingston said after the meeting that the county's computer use policy is relaxed and does not apply to elected officials.

"I think it needs to be clear to county employees what they can and can't do with their computers as far as emails and the internet is concerned," he said.

The investigation began when Glasscock forwarded a questionable email from its human resource director to Decatur Mayor Don Kyle. Kyle asked Glasscock not to forward such emails to him again. The incident later cost the human resource director his job.

"As things now stand, we can't function as a county government that is accountable to the people. That being the case, I think it's appropriate for me to ask Mr. Glasscock, our chairman, to resign."

— COUNTY COMMISSIONER STACY GEORGE

The commission acted on other matters as follows:

- Accepted a low bid of $141,581 from Tera Communications Inc. to furnish and install a microwave communications network for the Morgan County Emergency Management Communications District, from the Flint site to Brindlee Mountain, with payment to be made out of the Homeland Security Fund.
- Appointed election officials for the Jan.16 school tax election.
- Rescinded a hiring freeze resolution passed July 11, 2005, to now allow budgeted positions to be filled without commission approval in accordance with the existing adopted pay plan.
- Approved payment of $476 to Alfa Agency Alabama Inc. for a bond renewal for Russ Beard, Morgan County coroner, effective Jan.19 through Jan.19, 2011.
- Approved payment of $175 to Old Republic Surety Group for bond renewal for Ed Sims, effective March 1, 2007 through March 1, 2008.
- Approved payment of $125 to Hartselle Athletic Booster Club for a half-page advertisement in the Hartselle High School 2007 baseball program, payable out of the Tourism, Recreation and Convention Fund.
- Authorized the chairman to let bids on nine 2007 model police package vehicles for the Sheriff's Department, with five of them to be delivered as soon as possible and the other four after June 1.
- Approved certificates to subdivide and consolidate for Gregory and Pamela Nicholson and Jerry and Myra Oden and James and Rebecca Nicholson, Vaughn Bridge Road, District 2.

The Decatur Daily
THE INDEPENDENT VOICE OF THE TENNESSEE VALLEY SINCE 1912
SUNDAY, JANUARY 7, 2007

Hard drives, public records

Riverfront

The Decatur Daily
WEDNESDAY, MARCH 26, 2008
INSIDE: OBITUARIES, B5

Conflict over computers

Riverfront

The Decatur Daily

WEDNESDAY, APRIL [illegible]

INSIDE: OBITUARIES, B5

Commission questions hiring

Commissioners want sheriff to pay ex-data processing employee's salary, delay replacement

By Sheryl Marsh
smarsh@decaturdaily.com
340-2437

Morgan County Sheriff Greg Bartlett has various funds he can tap to cover the salary of a data processing employee if he wants one full time, a commissioner said.

One source is the jail store, where a pack of cigarettes reportedly costs $7 and Twinkies $3.

At a meeting Tuesday, commissioners delayed hiring a replacement employee for Ricky Brewer, who is now working

Commissioner Stacy George questions bills for attorney Bill Shinn's services, B5.

full time at the sheriff's office and jail. His former boss, David Hannah, manager of data processing, is continuing to pay his salary.

District 1 Commissioner Jeff Clark questioned whether Hannah needs to hire someone since Brewer spent 95 percent of his time working at the jail. Hannah said when Bartlett got his own computer servers Brewer spent a lot of time there, and during that time five servers that serve the rest of the county's computer system were neglected.

"He shouldn't have been over there that much," Hannah told the commission.

District 4 Commissioner

Please see Hiring, page B5

Hiring

From page B1

Stacy George agreed with Clark to delay hiring for Hannah's office until budget talks, but said there would be more talk about money that Bartlett controls.

George said the commission needs to look into the pistol permit fund that's under Bartlett's control and proceeds from the jail's store that the sheriff operates.

"We need to look at the sheriff paying his (Brewer's) salary," said George. "He's got plenty he can pay from."

George said inmates are paying "$7 for a pack of cigarettes and $3 for a Twinkie cake."

A pack of cigarettes at stores in the area costs about $4. Two Twinkies cost about 70 cents in a vending machine.

The manager of the jail store would not answer the phone when *The Daily* called to verify the prices. The employee who answered the phone said the manager said he could not release information because it had to come from the Sheriff's Department.

The sheriff's secretary said she would get the question about the prices to Bartlett, but he did not return a phone call.

Clark agreed that the sheriff should probably pay Brewer's salary. The commission did not vote on the item for Hannah hiring another employee and agreed to revisit the employment situation during budget talks.

Hannah fired Brewer on March 18 for an unauthorized trip he made with Bartlett and seven of his employees to New Orleans earlier this year. On appeal, the county's Personnel Review Board reinstated Brewer on April 4, but Hannah asked the commission to let him work for Bartlett. The commission gave unanimous approval.

EDITORIALS

The Decatur Daily
FRIDAY, JANUARY 26, 2007

It's time to stop stonewalling and release records to the public

The stonewalling against inspection of e-mails at the Morgan County Courthouse turns far more serious today. It's no longer a case of Commissioner Stacy George tilting at windmills, but one of elected officials attempting a legal end run around complying with state law.

The Morgan County Commission meets today at 1 p.m. in a work session and again at 2 p.m. Commissioners are expected to consider two proposals for which they used taxpayer money to pay an attorney to find a way to deny public records to taxpayers.

The effort is part of a national trend by public officeholders that accelerated after 9/11. Their basic philosophy is that the people of a democracy have no business knowing what government is doing. They know that open government makes them accountable to the public for their actions. They use national security and privacy as excuses to close public records and to shortcut the safeguards set up to protect everybody else's guaranteed rights.

Alabama law is clear about the public records the commission is sheltering. Most of them, by state law, are open for public inspection, including the e-mails on county computers at the courthouse.

Two proposals that County Attorney Bill Shinn drafted are anti-public. One amounts to any citizen having to ask to see specific e-mails, and would deny the public inspection of public records. The public would have to take a bureaucrat's word that the specified records do – or do not – exist. People wanting to inspect the records would have to bring their own computers on which to view them.

That is to discourage people from asking for records.

The other proposal sets a 50-cent fee for each copy of an e-mail, which could amount to a sizeable sum of money and could deny some people access because of their inability to pay. Anticipating somebody running up a big bill, the proposal calls for the person asking for the records to make a security deposit before getting the documents.

That's another attempt to discourage the public from asking to see public records.

Commissioner Jeff Clark is even talking about simply destroying records, which is against the law without following a strict process for doing so. Destroying the records, of course, could be a convenient way to deny Mr. George the e-mails he seeks. More than what Mr. George wants is at stake here.

Destroying public records illegally is punishable by a year in jail.

Whether you are on Mr. George's "side" or Sheriff Greg Bartlett's "side" or Revenue Commissioner Amanda Scott's "side" of the e-mail controversy doesn't matter. What's important is that county commissioners uphold due process and stop the stonewalling.

If the commission passes either of these policy options, doing so will invite statewide scrutiny and the matter will wind up in court. This policy is not about principle, but about holding the line on e-mails someone doesn't want the public to see for reasons that may or may not go beyond the line of duty.

This is about all of our rights, which should put all of us on the same side.

Articles listed in the Decatur Daily Archives

November 11, 2006-Racy e-mail incites probe
November 14, 2006-Outside firm to probe racy e-mail
November 15,2006-Morgan fires HR director over e-mail investigation
November 16, 2006-Lawyers to question employees in e-mail scandal at courthouse
November 29, 2006-Official seeks to erase hard drive, Morgan commissioner alleges
December 10, 2006-Courthouse confidential
December 13, 2006-Forensic expert probes e-mail
December 14, 2006-Letter tries to stop e-mail probe
December 15, 2006-Commissioner locks up hard drive; sheriff denies access
December 16, 2006-E-mail scandal: Scott changes locks on office
December 17, 2006-Scott, Bartlett win round 1 of Morgan e-mail scandal
December 18, 2006-Many readers disapprove of officials in e-mail probe
December 20, 2006-No free lawyers in e-mail battle
December 21, 2006-Morgan server bypassed
December 28, 2006-Morgan may vote on court order to get hard drives
December 29, 2006-George asks Glasscock to resign
January 5, 2007-Partial probe of e-mail OK with officials
January 7, 2007-Hard drives, public records
January 9, 2007-Probe yields more racy photos
January 10, 2007-Morgan e-mail probe is over
January 11, 2007-E-mail controversy not dead yet; disk goes to jail
January 12, 2007-Morgan employee won't show e-mail on server
January 18, 2007-E-mail issue in court
January 19, 2007-Scott in charge of hard-drive inspection
January 21, 2007-County commissioners should obey state law
January 23, 2007-Glasscock now concerned about sensitive information on county computer servers
January 25, 2007-New policy may cut records access
January 27, 2007-Morgan puts e-mail policy on hold
February 7, 2007-George's $4,500 secures records
February 8, 2007-George granted e-mail restraining order
February 11, 2007-Sheriff seeks U.S. inmates
February 13, 2007-Public view of e-mail may require 17-day wait
February 14, 2007-County e-mail on hold
February 15, 2007-E-mail list has Scott sending 2 in 75 days
February 22, 2007-George's attorney asks for recusal
February 25, 2007-Washing hands of e-mail, article #2 Bartlett:E-mails missing
February 27, 2007-Glasscock vows e-mail explanation Tuesday
February 28, 2007-Manager: Morgan e-mail not missing
March 1, 2007-Haddock staying in e-mail lawsuit
March 2, 2007-Manager can't recall if sheriff had e-mails now invisible
March 4, 2007-Who owns government office e-mails?
March 7, 2007-E-mail lawsuit challenged, article #2 Glasscock contacts ABI, FBI, on e-mails

March 14, 2007-Justifying $23,113 in overtime, article #2 Morgan e-mail hearing set for Friday.
March 16, 2007-Sheriff disciplines chief drug agent.
March 17, 2007-$250 an hour to probe e-mails.

THE DECATUR DAILY

Racy e-mail incites probe

Message made its way from Morgan courthouse to Decatur mayor

THE DECATUR DAILY

Outside firm to probe racy e-mail

George wants investigation with 'no ties to Morgan County politics'; more e-mails found

THE DECATUR DAILY

Lawyers to question employees in e-mail scandal at courthouse

THE DECATUR DAILY

Official seeks to erase hard drive, Morgan commissioner alleges

THE DECATUR DAILY

Forensic expert probes e-mail

Computer specialist in charge of investigation targeting elected officials, department heads, others

THE DECATUR DAILY

Letter tries to stop e-mail probe

Sheriff's lawyer claims office is exempt from computer investigation

THE DECATUR DAILY

Commissioner locks up hard drive; sheriff

THE DECATUR DAILY

E-mail scandal: Scott changes locks on office

THE DECATUR DAILY

Morgan server bypassed

Use of personal e-mail accounts makes hard-drive exams essential

THE DECATUR DAILY

George asks Glasscock to resign

E-mail probe won't include hard drives of Scott or Bartlett

THE DECATUR DAILY

Partial probe of e-mail OK with officials

Commissioners want closure in investigation

THE DECATUR DAILY

Hard drives, public records

Morgan personnel manual says all electronic records belong to county, but legal hassle remains

THE DECATUR DAILY

Probe yields more racy photos

THE DECATUR DAILY

E-mail issue in court

George seeks restraining order to allow him access; hosts changes tune on hard drive

By Evan Belanger

THE DECATUR DAILY

E-mail controversy not dead yet; disk goes to jail

By Sheryl Marsh

THE DECATUR DAILY

EDITORIAL

County commissioners should obey state law

THE DECATUR DAILY

Glasscock now concerned about sensitive information on county computer servers

By Sheryl Marsh

THE DECATUR DAILY

George granted e-mail restraining order

By Evan Belanger

THE DECATUR DAILY

County e-mail on hold

Restraining order issued to keep sheriff's servers headers from public

By Sheryl Marsh

THE DECATUR DAILY

George's $4,500 secures records

By Sheryl Marsh

THE DECATUR DAILY

George's attorney asks for recusal

Lawyer says Haddock, Glasscock serve together on corrections committee

By Sheryl Marsh

THE DECATUR DAILY

Bartlett: E-mails missing

Sheriff questions system's integrity; Glasscock says criminal probe possible

By Sheryl Marsh

THE DECATUR DAILY

Haddock staying in e-mail lawsuit

Judge refuses request to step aside from case

By Sheryl Marsh

THE DECATUR DAILY

Who owns government office e-mails?

2 Alabama legislators plan to introduce bill addressing complicated issue

By M.J. Ellington

GOV. BENTLEY: "WHO SANK MY GOVERNORSHIP"?

I fired six ethics complaint missiles striking the target with four hits and two misses. On April $5^{th,}$ 2017, the Alabama Ethics Commission reviewed the ethic complaints filed against Governor Bentley and found probable cause on several complaints. I spent approximately nine hours in a witness room during deliberation. Next, the Ethics Commission voted to turn the findings over to a former District Attorney in Montgomery County appointed by the new Attorney General. A few days later Governor Bentley decided to plead guilty to a couple of misdemeanor charges and agreement of reconciling certain violations. Governor Bentley agreed to repay debt along with doing community service. The last day of the Robert Bentley Governorship ended another paragraph in my book, but it started another.

This resignation by Governor Bentley because of these filed ethics complaints started a new chain of events that no one saw coming. The filing was just an old, wrinkled sheet of typing paper with no lines and the handwritten complaint against the Governor of Alabama by an old country boy from a community called Ryan. My original complaints are in this book signed, dated and a time of this event is on the original complaints. The findings of the Alabama Ethics Complaints are almost word for word as the original complaint I filed almost a year before the hearing. State Auditor Jim Zeigler had filed an original complaint as well. I looked carefully at his filing, and it was broad. It simply stated misuse of state resources and I knew to get a finding it had to be more specific. I filed 6 complaints and only 2 were dismissed. State Auditor Jim Ziegler held the heat on Governor Bentley in many ways other than his ethics complaint. He made issue of a beachfront Governor's Mansion and many more issues. Jim Zeigler, I consider a friend and a great State Auditor. As for the filings I made against former Governor Bentley it was not so easy. You see I work for the State of Alabama under the Commissioner of the Department of Corrections who is appointed by the Governor. This put me in a peculiar environment at my job as a Correctional Officer in the largest prison in Alabama.

The filing of the ethics complaints against former Governor Bentley and his pleading guilty with a resignation set into motion a chain of events that could not have occurred otherwise. This led to political discussions in an area involving the state and the nation. Elections took place that would never have happened without the initial filings. This chain of events ultimately pulled President Donald J. Trump to Alabama in a political fight with a total spending of just less than 20 million dollars for political advertising in Alabama. That boosted the economy and Alabama's profile as a state.

It is time to elaborate on this chain of events. The ethically challenged Governor Bentley resignation automatically put our rather unknown Lt. Governor Kay Ivey in the top spot in Alabama. Now, Governor Ivey took office removing some key appointments under the Bentley administration. Governor Ivey described this as steadying the ship in Alabama. She quickly reviewed state law and set a new date for the Special United States Senate Election of now newly appointed United States Attorney General Jeff Sessions. The state law is clear, and Governor Ivey followed the law. Former Governor Bentley had set the date of the primary for June of 2018, but Governor Ivey moved the new date to August 15$^{th.}$ of 2017. This changed the entire dynamics of the election and better reflected state law.

This special election had another fascinating result; Judge Roy Moore would now run for United States Senate instead of a speculated run for Governor of Alabama. I had always supported Judge Moore and he never goes away in politics. This maneuver ultimately put a large field of candidates in the GOP Primary and some on the Democrat side as well for this special election. The result was a Roy Moore victory over a former Governor Bentley appointed United States Senator Luther Strange in the Republican Primary. Strange is the way in which Alabama Attorney General Luther Strange was appointed to the position of United States Senator.

The way this appointment was made by former Governor Bentley who was being investigated by the very man he appointed big Luther Strange tainted the election of now United States Senator Luther Strange. Look how this chain of events following former Governor Bentley resigning had an everlasting effect on Alabama politics. Luther Strange lost to Roy Moore resulting in a magnitude of celebrities coming to Alabama for Roy Moore and President Trump coming to Alabama in a failed attempt to hold former Governor Bentley appointed Senator Luther Strange in the United States Senate.

As you see this is a great example of how you can make a difference in politics. You must have a backbone and you must be prepared to be called crazy. That is what corrupt politicians will try to do is paint you into being odd or strange. This eventually moves to just plain crazy. You must build good relationships with the media. You cannot go after too many issues at once. You must have facts that are easy to trace and easy to understand. If you lose the media and the people you will lose. Do not chase after fireflies just chase one until you catch it. Once you catch it the others will retreat for a season.

Jeremiah 51:20 & 23 NJKV

20 "You *are* My battle-ax *and* weapons of war:
For with you I will break the nation in pieces;
With you I will destroy kingdoms;

23 With you also I will break in pieces the shepherd and his flock;
With you I will break in pieces the farmer and his yoke of oxen;
And with you I will break in pieces governors and rulers.

Prison officer, former candidate Stacy George sounds off on governor's scandal

Gov. Robert Bentley faces possible prison time over ethics violations: What we know, what's next 1

Leada Gore

3

Ethics complaints 2

4

Alabama Gov. Robert Bentley resigns amid sex scandal

John Archibald

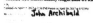

JESUS CHRIST
IS THE ANSWER

STATE OF ALABAMA
ETHICS COMMISSION

STATE OF ALABAMA
ETHICS COMMISSION

STATE OF ALABAMA
ETHICS COMMISSION

STATE OF ALABAMA
ETHICS COMMISSION

STATE OF ALABAMA
ETHICS COMMISSION

STATE OF ALABAMA
ETHICS COMMISSION

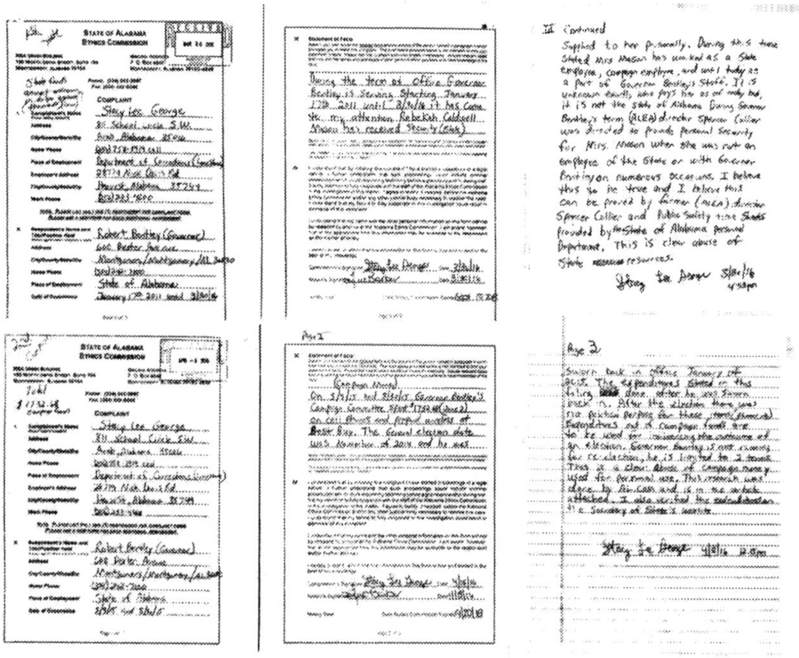

STATE OF ALABAMA
ETHICS COMMISSION

COMPLAINT

Stacy Lee George
811 School Circle S.W.
Arab, Alabama 35016
Department of Corrections
Robert Bentley (Governor)
600 Dexter Avenue
State of Alabama
January 17th 2011 until 3/30/16

Statement of Facts

During the term of office Governor Bentley is serving starting January 17th 2011 until 3/30/16 it has come to my attention Rebekah Caldwell Mason has received Security (ALEA)

II Continued

Supplied to her personally. During this time stated Mrs Mason has worked as a State employee, campaign employee, and until today as a part of Governor Bentley's Staff. It is unknown exactly who pays her as of today but, it is not the State of Alabama. During Governor Bentley's term (ALEA) director Spencer Collier was directed to provide personal Security for Mrs. Mason when she was not an employee of the State or with Governor Bentley on numerous occasions. I believe this to be true and I believe this can be proved by former (ALEA) director Spencer Collier and Public Safety time Sheets provided by the State of Alabama personnel Department. This is clear abuse of State resources.

Stacy Lee George 3/30/16 4:33pm

STATE OF ALABAMA
ETHICS COMMISSION

Total
$1752.68
Campaign Funds

COMPLAINT

Stacy Lee George
811 School Circle S.W.
Arab, Alabama 35016
Department of Corrections
Robert Bentley (Governor)
600 Dexter Avenue
State of Alabama
5/5/15 and 5/6/15

Page 1

Statement of Facts

(Campaign Money)
On 5/5/15 and 5/6/15 Governor Bentley's Campaign Committee spent $1752.68 (page 2) on cell phones and proprietary accessories at Best Buy. The General election date was November 4 of 2014 and he was

Page 2

Sworn back in office January of 2015. The expenditures stated in this filing were done after he was sworn back in. After the election there was no position pending for these items (personal) Expenditures out of campaign funds are to be used for influencing the outcome of an election. Governor Bentley is not running for re-election, he is limited to 2 terms. This is a clear abuse of campaign money used for personal use. This research was done by Al.com and is in the article attached. I also verified the information on the Secretary of State's website.

Stacy Lee George 4/5/16 12:13pm

3rd Campaign

STATE OF ALABAMA
ETHICS COMMISSION

Total
$ 70,[illegible]
Campaign Fund

COMPLAINT

Complainant's Name: Stacy Lee George
Address: 811 School Circle S.W.
City/County/State/Zip: Arab/Marshall/Alabama/35016
Home Phone: (256) 318-1923
Place of Employment: Department of Corrections (retired)
Employer's Address: 28779 Nick Davis Rd.
City/County/State/Zip: Harvest/LimeStone/Alabama 35749
Work Phone: (256) 233-4600

Respondent's Name and Title/Position Held: Robert Bentley (Governor)
Address: 600 Dexter Avenue
City/County/State/Zip: Montgomery/Montgomery/AL 36130
Home Phone: (334) 242-7100
Place of Employment: State of Alabama
Date of Occurrence: March 2015 to November 2015

Page 2

(Campaign Money)
March of 2015 to November of 2015
I show the following expenditures out of Governor Bentley's Campaign Committee: March 2015 - $18,[illegible]/
April 2015 - $ 7,[illegible]/ June 2015 - $ 6,[illegible]

Stacy Lee George 4/8/16
Sue Baker 4/8/16
4/20/18

Page 3

July 2015 $12,365.00/ September 2015 - $6,[illegible]
October 2015 - $ 6,[illegible]/November 2015 - $12,[illegible]
The General Election date was November of 2014 and he (Bentley) was sworn back in office January of 2015. The expenditures stated in this filing were done after he (Bentley) was sworn back in. After the election there was no political reason for these expenditures to (RCM) - a company owned by Mrs. Mason and her husband, Mr. Mason (she is already paid over 30K dollars from the State of Alabama). These expenditures range from polling to lodging, etc. Now, if Governor Bentley chose to go to the Republican National Convention in 4 months he could do so. Mrs Mason/Mr. Mason (RCM) would have no reason to be lodging anywhere now after the election. Furthermore, I do not see a need for polling data when the election is over, He is term limited so he cannot run again. Governor Bentley is neither trying to influence an election or on campaign business unless he is lodging with (RCM). (RCM) in my opinion was formed to funnel money for personal use. I believe the Bentley Campaign is the only one (RCM)

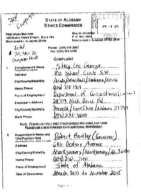

JESUS CHRIST
IS THE ANSWER

Page 4

is working on. This is clear abuse of campaign money used for personal gain. This research was done on the secretary of State's website.

Stacy Lee George 4/8/16 12:38pm

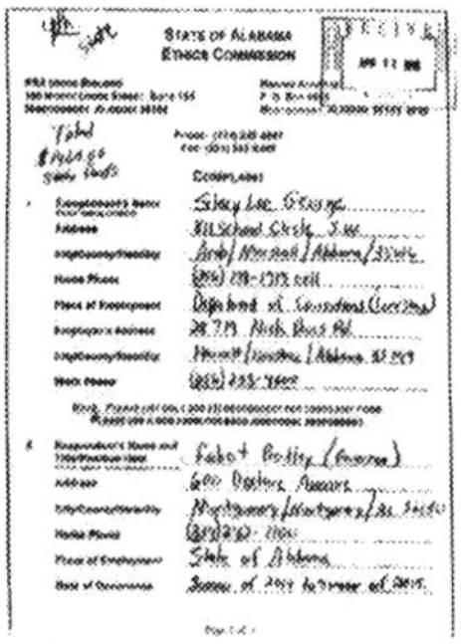

STATE OF ALABAMA
ETHICS COMMISSION

Stacy Lee George

Department of Corrections

Robert Bentley (Governor)

600 Dexter Avenue

State of Alabama

Summer of 2014 to Summer of 2015.

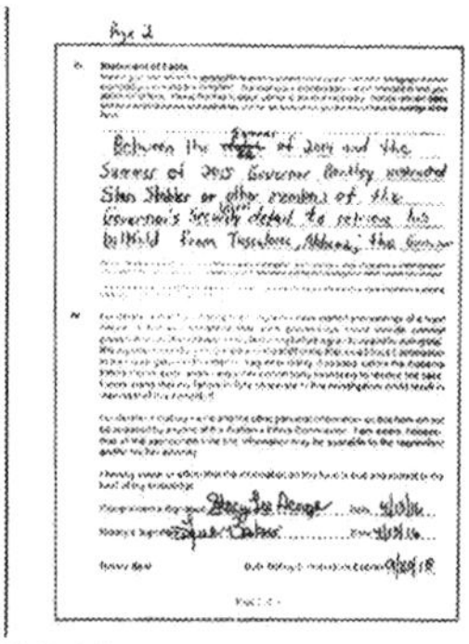

Page 2

Statement of Facts

Between the Summer of 2014 and the Summer of 2015 Governor Bentley instructed Stan Stabler or other members of the Governor's Security detail to retrieve his billfold from Tuscaloosa, Alabama, the Gover

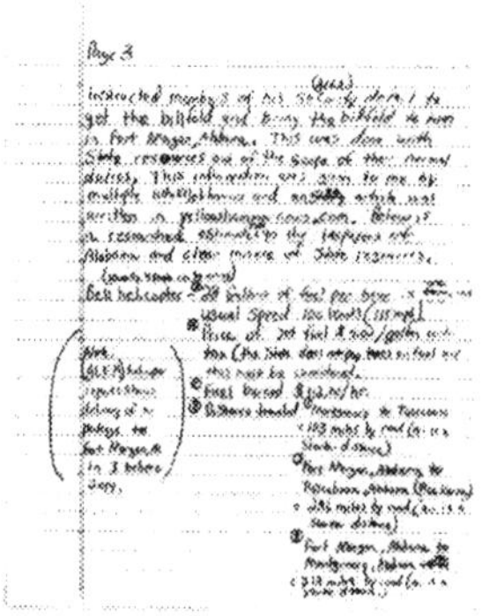

Page 3

instructed members of his security detail to get the billfold and bring the billfold to him in Fort Morgan, Alabama. This was done with State resources out of the scope of their normal duties. This information was given to me by multiple ... which was written in yellowhammer news.com. Below is a researched estimate to the taxpayers of Alabama and clear misuse of State resources.

Bell helicopter

Usual Speed 100 knots (115 mph)

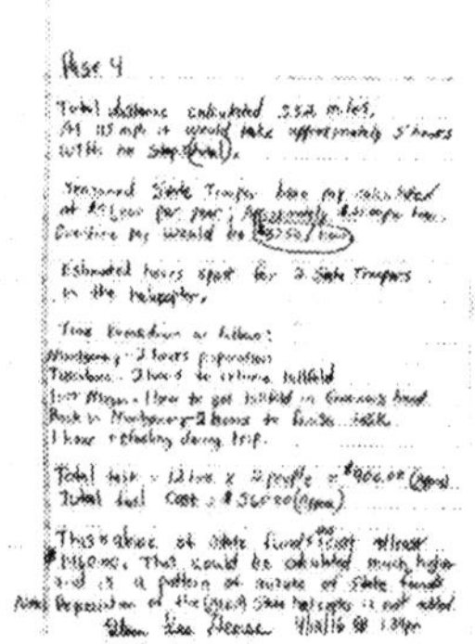

Page 4

Total distance calculated 552 miles.
At 115 mph it would take approximately 5 hours with no stops (total).

Seasoned State Trooper base pay calculated ... Therefore pay would be $37.50/hour.

Estimated hours spent for 2 State Troopers in the helicopter.

Time breakdown as follows:
Montgomery - 2 hours preparation
Tuscaloosa - 2 hours to retrieve billfold
Fort Morgan - 1 hour to get billfold in Governor's hand
Back to Montgomery - 2 hours to finish task
1 hour refueling during trip.

Total task = 12 hrs x 2 people = $900.00 (approx)
Total fuel cost = $560.00 (approx)

This is abuse of State funds at the least ... That could be calculated much higher and is a pattern of misuse of State funds.
Note: Depreciation of the (used) State helicopter is not added.

Stacy Lee George

JESUS CHRIST
IS THE ANSWER

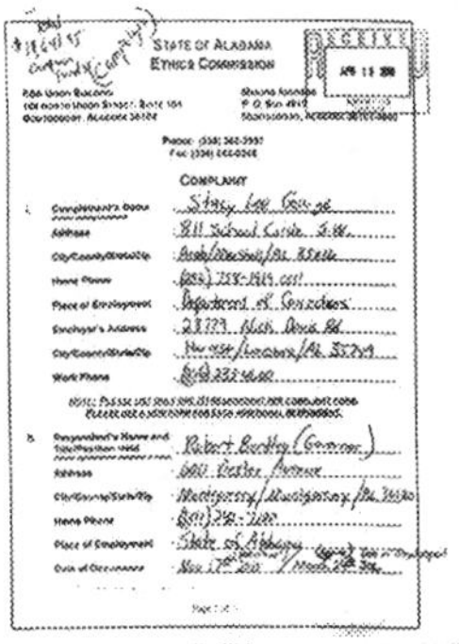

STATE OF ALABAMA
ETHICS COMMISSION

COMPLAINT

Complainant's Name	Stacy Lee George
Address	811 School Circle S.W.
City/County/State/Zip	Arab/Marshall/AL 35016
Home Phone	[illegible]
Place of Employment	Department of Corrections
Employer's Address	28779 Nick Davis Rd
City/County/State/Zip	Harvest/Limestone/AL 35749
Work Phone	[illegible]
Respondent's Name and Title/Position Held	Robert Bentley (Governor)
Address	600 Dexter Avenue
City/County/State/Zip	Montgomery/Montgomery/AL 36130
Home Phone	[illegible]
Place of Employment	State of Alabama
Date of Occurrence	Nov 17th 2015 / March 2nd 2016

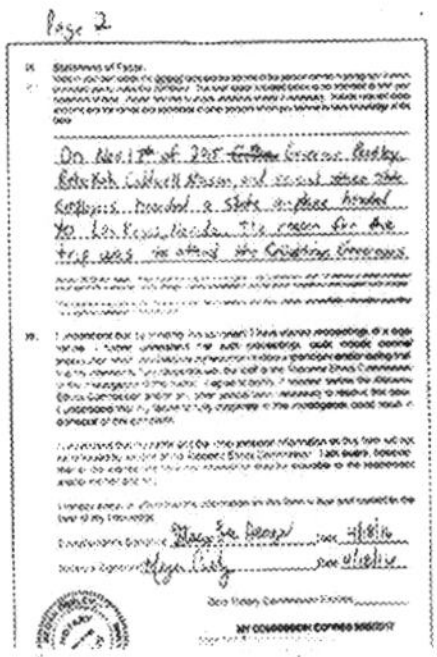

Page 2

Statement of Facts:

On Nov 17th of 2015 Governor Bentley, Rebekah Caldwell Mason, and several other State employees boarded a State airplane headed to Las Vegas, Nevada. The reason for the trip was to attend the Republican Governors

Complainant's Signature: Stacy Lee George Date: 4/8/16

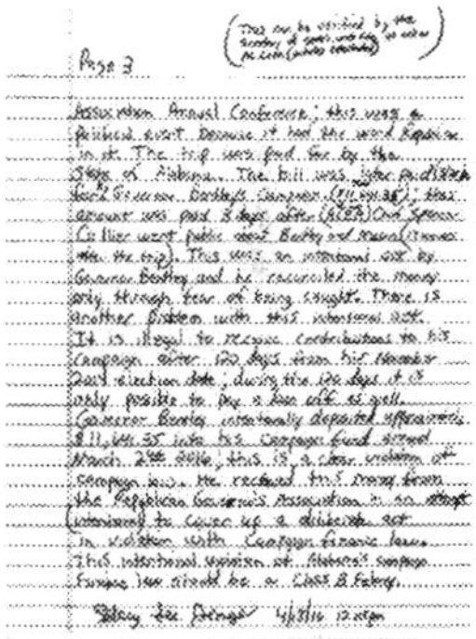

Page 3

Association Annual Conference; this was a political event because it had the word Republican in it. The trip was paid for by the State of Alabama. The bill was later paid back with Governor Bentley's Campaign ($11,644.35); this amount was paid 3 days after (AL.com) and Spencer Collier went public about Bentley and Mason (3 months after the trip). This was an intentional act by Governor Bentley and he reconciled the money only through fear of being caught. There is another problem with this intentional act. It is illegal to receive contributions to his campaign after 120 days from his November 2014 election date; during the 120 days it is only possible to pay a loan off as well. Governor Bentley intentionally deposited approximately $11,644.35 into his Campaign fund around March 2nd 2016; this is a clear violation of campaign law. He received this money from the Republican Governor's Association in an attempt (intentional) to cover up a deliberate act in violation with Campaign finance laws. This intentional violation of Alabama's campaign finance law should be a Class B Felony.

Stacy Lee George 4/8/16

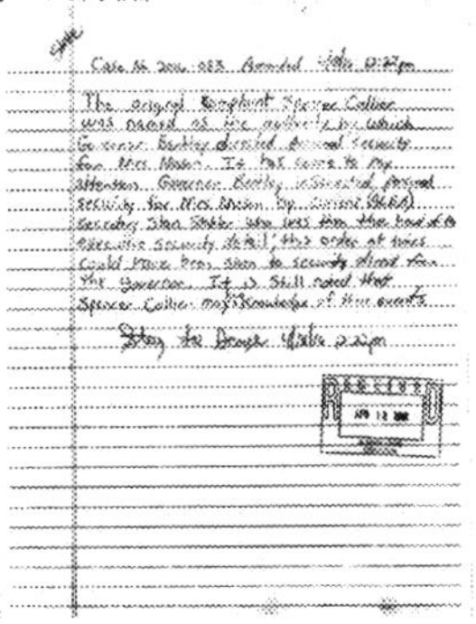

Case # 2016-083 Amended 4/12/16

The original complaint Spencer Collier was named as the authority by which Governor Bentley directed personal security for Mrs. Mason. It has come to my attention Governor Bentley instructed personal security for Mrs. Mason by current (ALEA) Secretary Stan Stabler who was then the head of the Executive Security detail; this order at times could have been seen to security detail from the Governor. It is still noted that Spencer Collier may have knowledge of these events.

Stacy Lee George 4/12/16

JESUS CHRIST
IS THE ANSWER

JESUS CHRIST
IS THE ANSWER

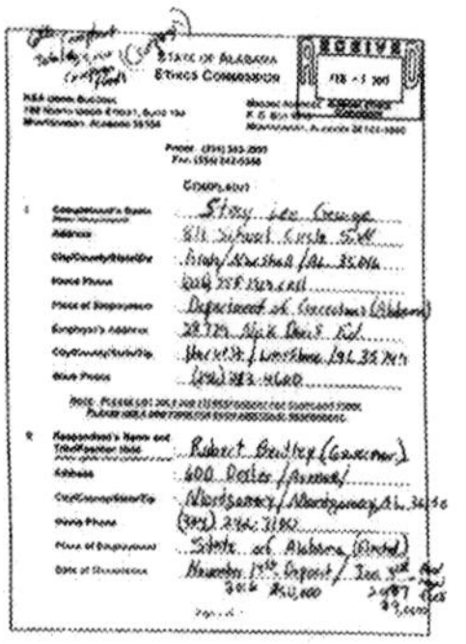
State of Alabama
Ethics Commission

Complaint

Stacy Lee George

Robert Bentley (Governor)

State of Alabama (Elected)

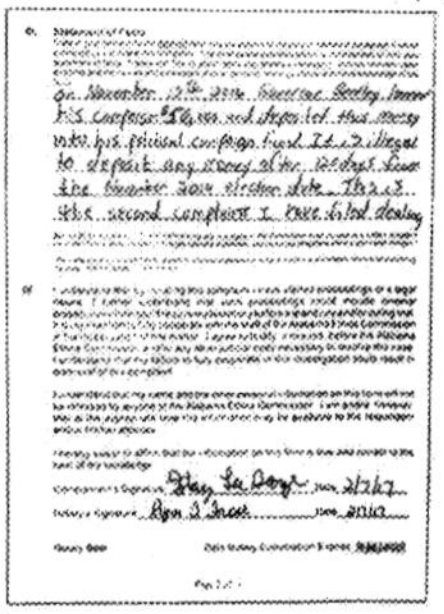
Statement of Facts

On November 12th 2016 Governor Bentley loaned his campaign $50,000 and deposited this money into his political campaign fund. It is illegal to deposit any money after 120 days from the November 2014 election date. This is the second complaint I have filed dealing

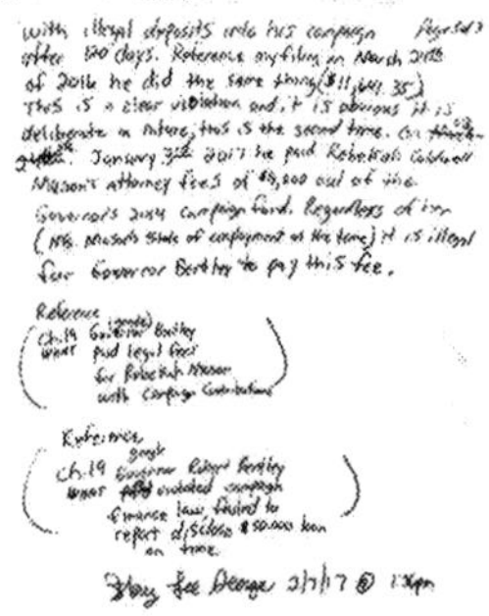
with illegal deposits into his campaign after 120 days. Reference my filing in March of 2016 he did the same thing ($11,644.35). This is a clear violation and it is obvious it is deliberate in nature, this is the second time. On January 3rd 2017 he paid Rebekah Caldwell Mason's attorney fees of $9,000 out of the Governor's 2014 campaign fund. Regardless of [illegible] (Ms. Mason's state of employment at the time) it is illegal for Governor Bentley to pay this fee.

Reference
Ch. 19 Governor Bentley
what paid legal fees for Rebekah Mason with Campaign Contributions

Reference
Ch. 19 Governor Robert Bentley
what violated campaign finance law, failed to report disclose $50,000 loan on time.

Stacy Lee George 2/7/17 @ 1:30pm

1

IN THE DISTRICT COURT FOR THE FIFTEENTH JUDICIAL CIRCUIT
MONTGOMERY COUNTY, ALABAMA

STATE OF ALABAMA, Plaintiff, v. ROBERT J. BENTLEY, Defendant.	)	Case No. [illegible]

Governor [illegible] Plea Agreement

PLEA AGREEMENT

Come now the State of Alabama, by and through Supernumerary District Attorney Ellen J. Brooks appointed by the Attorney General pursuant to Section 12-17-216 of the Code of Alabama as Special Assistant Attorney General, and the Defendant, by and through his attorney, and agree to the following terms, each of which is an essential part of the parties' agreement:

1. No later than April 10, 2017, the Defendant will enter a plea of guilty, stating under oath sufficient facts to support his guilty pleas, to each of two complaints:

   A. Complaint 1 – Failing to File a Major Contribution Report – Ala. Code Section 17-5-8.1(a), a Class A misdemeanor

   B. Complaint 2 – Knowingly Converting Campaign Contributions to Personal Use Ala. Code Section 36-25-6, a Class A misdemeanor

2. Sentencing will occur immediately after the acceptance of the guilty pleas; the pre-sentence report will be waived; the duration of the sentence and the determination of probation will be at the discretion of the Court; as part of his sentence the Defendant will do the following:

   A. Pay the following within 1 week of sentencing:

   (1) $100 ($50 per complaint) assessment to the Alabama Crime Victims

2

Compensation Commission,

   (2) Full court costs for both complaints,

   (3) Fines of $3000 to Complaint 1 and of $3000 to Complaint 2.

   B. Reimburse the campaign fund $8,912.00 within 1 week of sentencing.

   C. Surrender all campaign funds (approximately $36,912.00) to the State of Alabama within 1 week of sentencing.

   D. Render at least 100 hours of community service in his capacity as a licensed physician to the people of the State of Alabama within the terms of his sentence.

3. The Defendant will resign from his position as Governor of the State of Alabama by letter no later than 1 hour before pleading guilty and provide the State of Alabama with a copy of that resignation letter before pleading guilty.

4. The Defendant will not seek or serve in any public office.

5. The Defendant will waive any retirement or other benefits to which he would otherwise be entitled, including but not limited to benefits under Ala. Code §§ 36-13-13 and 36-33-2.

6. The Defendant will waive any and all objections to venue and his right to appeal any issue.

7. By signing this document, the Defendant represents that he is an adult, is competent to enter into this agreement and plead guilty, is satisfied with the work of his attorney, has been advised of his rights by his attorney, and that he intelligently, knowingly, and voluntarily agrees with the terms of the Plea Agreement.

8. The parties agree that this plea agreement resolves all potential state criminal charges against the Defendant based on pending investigations, including the

3

referrals from the Alabama Ethics Commission and the matters referenced in the Pre-Hearing Submission of Special Counsel to the House Judiciary Committee dated April 7, 2017.

Agreed this 10th day of April, 2017.

Robert J. Bentley Defendant	Ellen J. Brooks Special Assistant Attorney General
William C. Athanas Attorney for Defendant	Miles M. Hart Deputy Attorney General Chief, Special Prosecutions Division

A BLOODY BATTLE UNTIL THE END OVER ACCESS TO PUBLIC RECORDS

People might wonder why I would put the most important chapter last. I want to leave you the reader with the most important task at hand in government and that is simply be a good gadfly always asking questions. This war began in November of 2000 a week after I was sworn in, and it was like a cool breeze outside. It was blistering hot inside the Morgan County Commission meetings, and it was like a furnace until November of 2008 when I exited the courthouse. My seat was District number four on the end as seated at commission meetings. As I glanced to my right, I could see that I was clearly outnumbered being the only Republican in the group at the start. The key element was true diligence and tenacious reporting by the Press. Throughout this gruesome war I thought to myself please GOD give me the courage to defend access to public records because I am the only person on the commission that really seems to care most of the time. My only weapon was an ink pen that never ran out of ink, and I like to call it the Press. Without good reporting of facts this book could not have been written.

There is a reason Access to Public records is my most important chapter. I will say it again. Without access to public records this book could not have been written. Through access to public records what could have been just a fairytale is really a brutal nightmare come to fruition. Access to Public Records is in my opinion as follows: the right to obtain a written account of facts by a group of people sharing a common interest. That common interest is accountability. I get tired of people talking about accountability and doing nothing to protect it. I put my money where my mouth is, and I have a written printed account of it. I try to stay away from boastful speaking throughout my book, but this is one battle I will brag about. I will also attempt to instill the importance of the Press too. You may not agree with the Press leaning liberal on a lot of national issues and some state issues as well. Dealing with corruption the Press is on point in the many news outlets printed in this book. Corruption smolders in the dark and not one person reading this despite their political philosophy likes corrupt business done in the dark.

Throughout my tenure on the county commission, I kept things public in a creative manner at times. To my knowledge before I was elected to the commission people were in the dark and the newspaper articles disappeared shortly after my departure in 2008. Some things are in place for a generation or until the generation forgets. My time on Earth is limited, but this book will live on forever. My hope is this book serves as a reminder of what goes on in all levels of government when nobody is watching. I think with a large circulation of this book in the hands of taxpayers present in every county throughout the state of Alabama this book will keep a few crooks somewhat honest. This book could also help the entire United States of America.

There would be no need to have a written account of things if everyone's heart followed this scripture.

2 Corinthians 3:2-3

2 You are our epistle written in our hearts, known and read by
all men; 3 clearly you are an epistle of Christ, ministered by us,
written not with ink but by the Spirit of the living God, not
on tablets of stone but on tablets of flesh, *that is,* of the heart.

DECATUR DAILY

Thursday, March 25, 2004

Bennich puts grip on open records

Requests for files wanted 2 to 3 days in advance

By Sheryl Marsh
Staff Writer

Just weeks after THE DAILY sued public officials to report on hundreds of phone calls between two county officials and a delay in returning travel advances, Morgan County Commission Chairman Larry Bennich is clamping down on access to records.

Rather than making the records immediately available, Bennich is requiring individuals to ask the county administrator who informs him of the requests he has approved.

Any requests for records must be made two to three days in advance. County Administrator Willa Dockery said the response time will depend on whether the records are in this office or referred to archives.

Dennis Bailey, general counsel for the Alabama Press Association, said the officials are bordering on being unreasonable.

'Pushing the envelope'

"It's probing the envelope on what's reasonable because when you have to get approval from the highest level of any organization to get something as simple as pay records for public employees, you're eventually going to have situations where those are delays," Bailey said.

"It shouldn't take three to four days to get these records and these situations usually end up in the courts. They are going to find it difficult to do without always bluntly refusing of requests are made and can be handled without having to clear

Please see Records, page A4

THE DECATUR DAILY

RIVERFRONT C1

CLASSIFIED

Tuesday, November 27, 2001

JESUS CHRIST
IS THE ANSWER
Jesus Christ is the Answer #3

Morgan looking to control access to public records

By Sheryl Marsh
Daily Staff Writer

Morgan County Commission Chairman Larry Bennich is trying to regulate the public's access to county records by creating a policy that requires residents to fill out a request form and wait up to three days.

County attorney Bill Shinn presented the proposed policy during a commission work session Monday and a resolution to adopt it was on the meeting agenda but was removed after Commissioner Stacy George opposed part of it.

Commissioners will address it again in the future.

The kind of documents involved in Bennich's effort includes travel records that the news media uses to tell taxpayers how their money is being spent. Occasionally, citizens request

records also but Bennich decided that any particular request for documents prompted him to have Shinn create the proposed policy.

Bennich said he asked Shinn to draft the policy to establish a cost for making copies of documents.

"We have people come in from time to time so we need to know what to charge for copies. We don't have a policy and I think we need one."

Bennich said after the meeting. But the chairman's proposal goes beyond cost to include bureaucratic steps that could delay access to records.

The policy would require anyone from the public to fill out a request form and state the reason for wanting to see the information. Commission office staff may ask those who want to look at records to come back at another time if it is not practical for them to provide

Please see Morgan, page C4

Larry Bennich Stacy George
Chairman Commissioner

Records

Continued from page A1

with higher authorities," he added.

The change comes three weeks after District 4 Commissioner Stacy George removed phone and travel records of various offices Dockery made the change known this week after George questioned mileage and unreconciled travel advances during a meeting Monday.

Bennich and Dockery said the change has nothing to do with that matter and they are not trying to hide anything in the records.

"It's to bring efficiency back to the office," said Bennich. "Everybody and his neighbor are not going around any of the departments. So that are unnecessarily and send the ladies to get something

for them and this hinders them from doing their work.

Although his method of improving efficiency is adding an extra step for him and workers, Bennich said it will not cause delays and he or Dockery will determine the time when the person requesting the records get them.

"I've got an office to run up here to conduct business and these ladies pay a vital role in that," Bennich said. "They need to be able to do their work."

He acknowledged, however, that the employees did not complain about getting records for the public.

Alabama law says, "Every citizen has a right to inspect and take a copy of any public writing of this state, except as otherwise expressly provided by statute."

Bennich said he is not trying to defy the law and will not try to withhold information from the media.

"The newspaper is our best source to the public and we want the public to know what's going on," he said.

Dockery said if she and Bennich are absent, the deputy administrator will be in charge and she would contact Bennich when requests are made for records.

Hundreds of phone calls

George faxed 225 telephone calls made from Revenue Commissioner Amanda Scott's office to Jackson County Revenue Commissioner Ron Crawford's office within a year THE DAILY also had communications with employees by mail his feelings from receiving his feelings.

When George questioned the calls, Bennich accused him of trying to "run down" what he has built with employees by making his file findings from THE DAILY.

THE DAILY obtained George's

Dennis Bailey, general counsel for the Alabama Press Association, said the test of such a policy is in the way it is implemented — whether it is used to deny or delay access to information that previously was public.

Bailey also cited a 1981 opinion by the Alabama attorney general that says that custodians of the records may charge for copies, but should supply them free if possible. If "budgetary constraints" make a fee necessary, the fee should be nominal, covering the agency's costs, the attorney general said.

George said during the work session that he's against with holding information from the public about elected officials, but he favors personnel matters being private.

"I want to make sure we don't try to protect elected officials," he said. "We don't need to put up a shield to try to keep them from knowing what we are doing As for charging for copies, I think we need to charge only if they want an excessive number of documents and I don't think we should charge the media at all."

George said he wants time to study the policy but said he will not agree to parts of it that he opposes.

Commissioners Don Stisher and Jeff Clark acknowledged that when they ran for office they vowed to make sure records and meetings are open to the public, but they favor the policy and believe taxpayers should pay for copies. Commissioner Faye Sparkman, who was appointed to complete her husband's term, agrees with the policy also and the three said they will vote to adopt it.

Bennich said he has no problem with supplying records to the newspaper and other media.

"I think we will deal with the media as quick as we possibly can." he said. "I don't see anything that will change. More than anything else, I just want to make sure the ladies in the office know what's going on and how much to charge."

Stisher recommended taking the item off the agenda for Monday's meeting so the commission can study it and perhaps get input from the media.

Morgan

Continued from page C1

records immediately. The staff may take up to three working days to make the records available.

The policy would also require payment of fees for copies of documents obtained by those seeking public records. Copies from the public book, which are 11-by-17 inches, will cost $1, legal-size copies, 33 cents; and letter size, 25 cents.

Shinn said most records are public but some are not, such as personnel records, which list personal information like Social Security numbers. The policy would prohibit disclosure of those records as well as records of personnel investigations. Records from investigations will be available to those involved after the investigation is finished.

The proposed policy requires county personnel to consult the county attorney before they deny access to public records

bard's phone records from the Jackson County Commission office, which showed he made 118 calls to Decatur.

Scott and Crawford said they called each other hundreds of times to discuss an aerial photography project.

After reporters finished searching the records in Jackson County Commission Chairman James Tidmore worked there for not giving him a specific reason for getting the records.

Bailey said Tidmore law states that public officials can ask for a reason, but when reporters kept telling their positions that is a valid short reason.

The reason does not have to be much more than "I'm a reporter." Reporters have to say they're working on a story. But he said Tidmore should be enough.

Both Morgan and Jackson counties changed their policies

on releasing records after THE DAILY reported its findings.

Tidmore said Tuesday that the Jackson commissioners adopted a resolution increasing the cost for copies of documents from 10 cents to 50 cents and requiring those seeking records to come plete a form.

The Daily Sentinel in Scotts boro reported the policy states that anyone requesting records must give a legitimate "public purpose" for the request.

Dockery said she and Bennich did not coordinate the change in Morgan with Jackson County although she acknowledged talking to Tidmore the day the DAILY reporters were in Scottsboro.

Dockery said Tidmore called and asked her why they were there and she told him about those and she told him it asked have been requesting the story about the phone calls between the revenue commissioner

he could read the story on the Internet.

No gag order

Dockery said the change is not to keep employees from talking to people or the media members who come to the office because she realizes the county cannot violate the workers' constitutional right of freedom of speech.

"There is no gag order. No reason we can't do that," she said.

George said he requested a record Wednesday and Dockery told him that all requests must go through Bennich

"I told Ms Dockery that if I need a record, I'm not going to ask Mr Bennich I'm going to center (call it myself." George said He said Dockery finally gave him the record he requested.

"Any changes to public access to records should be made by the commissioners passing a resolution, not by Mr Bennich"

THE DECATUR DAILY

RIVERFRONT B1

Sunday, November 23, 2003

Setting meeting agendas

Chairman Bennich can't reject items, block motions

By Sheryl Marsh
DAILY Staff Writer

Morgan County Commission Chairman Larry Bennich cannot reject items that commissioners want to put on a meeting agenda, as he did recently, nor can he stop commissioners from making motions from the floor.

He has the authority to prepare the agenda and preside over commission meetings; however, if the commission does not vote to adopt the agenda of each meeting, it is merely a guide for the meeting, according to Robert's Rules of Order.

Regardless of the rules, Bennich said, he still wants to meet in private with a commissioner before allowing items on the agenda.

State law requires Bennich and commissioners to meet and discuss business in public unless it involves the good name and character of a person.

'Discuss things'

"I've never denied putting anything on the agenda. All I asked them to do is discuss things with me," Bennich said. "If they want to bring up stuff on personnel and certain departments, they need to research and think about that a little bit."

Before the Nov. 10 meeting, District 4 Commissioner Stacy George asked personnel in the commission office to put an item on the agenda so the commission could vote on putting the security operation under the sheriff's administration.

His request came after THE DAILY reported that security supervisor Ed Stone made $18,000 in overtime in about nine months.

Bennich said at the meeting that he did not allow the item on the agenda because he is satisfied with the way security is operating. Later, he said George should have discussed the issue with him before trying to put it on the agenda. George asked County

Larry Bennich
Commission chairman

Stacy George
District 4 commissioner

Attorney Bill Shinn to get a legal opinion about whether Bennich can keep commissioners from putting items on the agenda.

Please see Agenda, page B4

Agenda

Continued from page B1

Shinn issued the opinion last week.

He said no law governs commission meetings, therefore the commission operates under Robert's Rules of Order.

"At the beginning of the meeting, the chairman asks for a vote on whether or not to adopt the proposed agenda as the agenda for the meeting," Shinn stated in the opinion. "A majority of the members present and voting can adopt the proposed agenda for the meeting. If a proposed agenda is not formally adopted by the meeting to which it applies, it is not binding as to what may or may not be considered by the meeting.

"Presumably, any relevant business of the county could be introduced by motion and seconded, and voted upon in such a situation."

He stated that the appropriate way to put a non-agenda matter to a vote would be to wait until the commission completes all other business matters.

George said he is glad to hear that Bennich cannot dictate what he wants on the agenda.

"I feel confident that in the future anything can be brought up from the floor at the end of a commission meeting," George said. "He (Bennich) does have somewhat control of the agenda for day-to-day operations, but that's it. In the future he will not stop a motion from being made from the floor." Both George and District 3 Commissioner John Glasscock said Bennich has stopped them from making motions from the floor.

"He did it two meetings ago," said Glasscock. "My understanding of the agenda for the meeting is that any commissioner can add an item to the agenda without the permission of the chairman or anyone else."

As for the security issue, George said, he did not try to get it on the agenda for Monday's meeting, but he plans to discuss it and the situation dealing with county license inspectors of the sales tax office carrying guns.

District 1 Commissioner Jeff Clark said the commission should communicate better.

"I think the most important thing is an open line of communication between the commissioners and the chairman," he said. "Respect from both sides would eliminate all the problems that we've had. The commission has nothing to hide in the meetings, and I think it would benefit everyone to communicate. Everybody is talking, but not to each other."

George says he wants to help public awareness

By Sheryl Marsh
DAILY Staff Writer

Morgan County District 4 Commissioner Stacy George said he plans to continue his trend of being accountable to the public while working to move the county forward.

Stacy George
Morgan County District 4 Commissioner

George, 35, seeks re-election for a second term on the County Commission. He faces challengers Tom Kennemer and Terry Brown in the June 1 Republican primary.

"I would like to continue as I've done in the past, making the county better through working with schools, sharing with them by building facilities such as the four athletic fields at Brewer High School," George said. "I also want to continue to make the public aware of what's going on with their government and, as we find problems, I want to work with the commission to put measures in place to resolve them as I have done in the past."

Please see George, page C3

George

Continued from page C1

He said he is pleased with what he has accomplished, especially putting walking trails around all five schools in his district and paving roads.

"As a whole, I feel like I've been able to bring a welcome change to county government in the form of openness and fairness which led to accountability and saving taxpayers' money. In the future, if we continue on course, I do not see a need to raise any additional taxes in the county," George said.

While George has faced opposition from some party leaders in Morgan County and he campaigned against GOP Gov. Bob Riley's failed $1.2 billion tax hike, he gained endorsements Tuesday from the Republican Assembly and Conservative Christians of Alabama, two statewide organizations.

Turnout

The groups provide support for candidates whom they endorse by encouraging a turnout of voters in their favor. In addition, the Republican Assembly prints flyers and pays for newspaper advertisement for its chosen candidates.

A native of Morgan County, George is a 1987 graduate of Brewer High. He attended Calhoun Community College, where he studied political science. During his tenure as commissioner, George completed the county commission college by taking courses in Birmingham, Montgomery and Auburn.

WHAT ABOUT THE SPIRITUAL POLITICAL BATTLE GOING ON IN THE AIR?

We have spent a lot of time discussing earthly political battles. I would do you an injustice if I did not at least open a door for you into the battle between spiritual good and evil in the air. We are Chess pieces in a game of life here on Earth between the Body of Christ and the Body of satan. There is a real war going on and you MUST pick a side. By staying out of the battle you have chosen your side; the side is the kingdom of satan.

In the past three years I have learned so much about the ways satan and his goons(demons) affect our daily lives. I will not go into a lot of detail, that is the next book. Here are a few details about breaking generational bloodline curses on every human being alive including preachers, evangelists, prophets, apostles, teachers, inmates in prison, and yes YOU. I have witnessed three demons expelled using the anointed card below. I have witnessed drug addiction broken immediately. I have witnessed people touching this anointed card and uncontrollable physical movements happen. I have witnessed people falling in the floor while reading this notecard.

This notecard developed as I read a lifechanging book-Issuing Divine RESTRAINING ORDERS from the Courts of Heaven by Dr. Francis Myles with Robert Henderson. I was introduced to Dr. Francis Myles when my wife Karen encouraged me to watch Dr. Myles on the Sid Roth Show called, "It's Supernatural". Next, Kevin Zadai appeared on the Sid Roth show and I picked up on personal things about Jesus that I used in my development of thinking. Let us not stop now. Another person came into play.

Kynan Bridges comes on the Sid Roth show, and as I start watching him, he articulates kingdom principals involved in spiritual warfare. Tracy Cooke comes on the show; it absolutely amazes me that a skateboarder can turn into a prophet. This lets me know how GOD uses a diverse group of people. I just recommend you subscribe to Sid Roth and watch his various videos of so many anointed people, so you understand that supernatural things of GOD occur.

This notecard described: The first four lines are italicized, and this is the renewing of your mind. This must be done sometimes 5 or more times per day depending on your environment. I would say more for new Christians, but that would be **incorrect**. The next four lines are the breaking of generational bloodline curses. Dr. Francis Myles book is the pattern I used for this. His book is very simple in this regard, and it works great. This needs to be read once per week. The next three lines are somewhat unique. The Holy Spirit revealed to me that a person's first name means something. My name Stacy means biblically, "Resurrection or restore to life". Did you know your first name was given to you by GOD? Your last name is your father's bloodline name. Your parents think they gave you your first name, but I do not think so. Lastly, it is important you are baptized in the Holy Spirit/ Holy Ghost. It is also important that your spiritual gifts are activated. All these activities are done in the reading of this card OUT LOUD, OUT LOUD, and OUT LOUD. You must SPEAK things into existence. I have literally performed hundreds of deliverances of people by saying repeat after me with this card. The more people repeating in agreement the more powerful it is. At the end, when in person, I speak my spirit language and I know of two things that happen. Angels of GOD come into the area and demons of satan are bound casting them out of the area. This is somewhat a temporary restraining order if you will. I do not understand the mysteries of GOD, I only know this is powerful, especially in person.

As you read this card OUT LOUD while glancing in a mirror you will physically see your face relax and your eyes go from wide open to almost shut at the end. This happens 100 percent of the time. I have witnessed this hundreds of times over the last year and a half.

READ this notecard OUT LOUD and feel free to use this card any way you need to. This is an anointed prayer and satan will try every way possible to stop you from reading this. Remember there is a political battle on the ground and in the air. You need to be a warrior for Jesus Christ and the Kingdom of GOD. GOD has an amazing retirement plan called Heaven. See you there someday.

THIS IS THE NOTECARD BELOW THAT IS MENTIONED IN PRIOR TEXT

BREAK YOURSELF FREE FROM GENERATIONAL CURSES; IT IS EASY! THIS MUST BE READ OUT LOUD!

Dear Heavenly Father," I ask that you forgive me of the sins I know of and the sins I do not know of so that you will hear my prayer. I release all offense of insult/anger/pride/depression/ unforgiveness/ bitterness/ jealously/selfishness /resentment/fear/anxiety and everything else that is not of GOD that I have in me; I repent in the name of Jesus Christ, forgive me Lord".

HEAVENLY FATHER, I repent for all covenants with demons that have existed in my ancestral bloodline. Lord, I ask that any agreement with demons would be rescinded. Lord, any demonic right to claim my bloodline and me is now dismissed before Your courts in Jesus' name. Thank You Lord, for revoking these demonic covenants and altars in Jesus' mighty name! *Prayer from the author inspired by the Holy Spirit,* "I pray that you are RESTORED to LIFE spiritually, mentally, and physically; also, I pray that you receive the Holy Spirt including activation of your spiritual gifts in the name of Jesus Christ". Just say, "I accept in Jesus name".

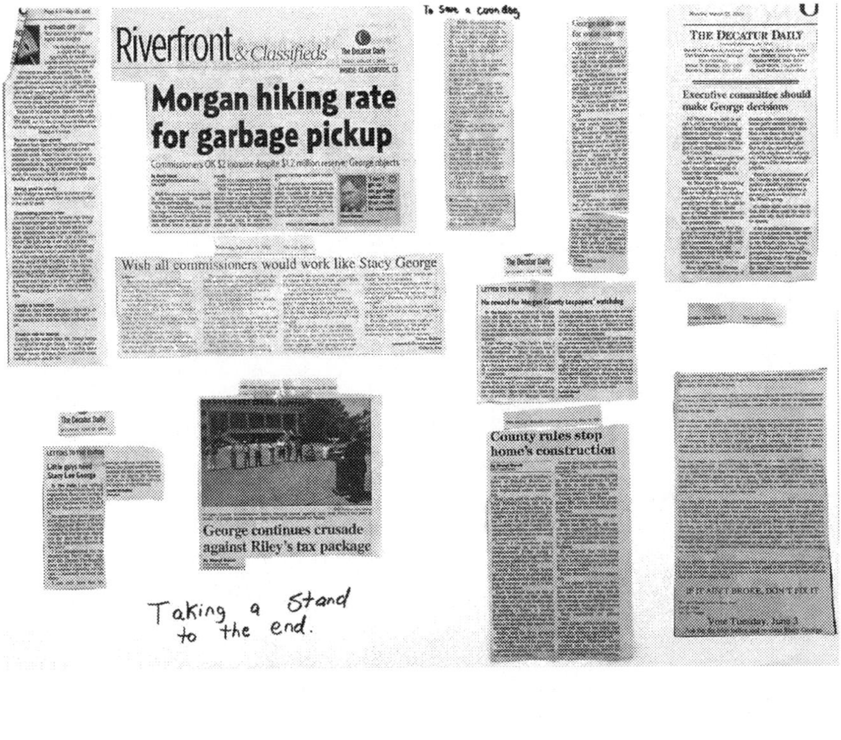
To save a coon dog
Riverfront & Classifieds
The Decatur Daily
Morgan hiking rate for garbage pickup
Wish all commissioners would work like Stacy George
The Decatur Daily
Executive committee should make George decisions
The Decatur Daily
No reward for Morgan County taxpayers' watchdog
The Decatur Daily
Little guys need Stacy Lee George
George continues crusade against Riley's tax package
County rules stop home's construction
IF IT AIN'T BROKE, DON'T FIX IT
Vote Tuesday, June 3
Taking a stand to the end.

Commissioner Stacy George hires fired Morgan sheriff employee

Hire

Continued from page C1

Four practice fields slated for construction

Fields

Fine arts donation

1st black woman fills water board

Water

Continued from page C1

JESUS CHRIST
IS THE ANSWER
Jesus Christ is the Answer

Accomplishments

Riverfront
George to run for governor
The Arab Tribune
Stacy George running for Ala. governor
Race for state's top office heating up
The Arab Tribune
Arab man part of downfall
Ethics
George to officially announce in Selma
George
Recap 2014 and 2018
JESUS CHRIST IS THE ANSWER

Tuesday, June 3rd Let George Do It...

Re-Elect Stacy Lee

GEORGE

Morgan Co. Comm. Countywide

The People's Voice on the Morgan County Commission

It's Your Money, It's Your Choice,
Let George Do It Again
I'll Continue To Be Your Voice!

One of our biggest accomplishments for East Morgan County is working with Sue Baker Roan to create the East Morgan County Tag Office.

www.stacygeorge.com

STACY GEORGE

Republican

"County Commission"

District 4

stacygeorge@mindspring.com

We Need A Conservative Voice
in Morgan County

(256) 586-2529
Pager: 309-8143

STACY GEORGE

Re-Elect Let George Do It...

Stacy Lee

GEORGE

Morgan Co. Comm. District 4

www.stacygeorge.com

Blast from
the Past.

Carrying the Cross 1.3 miles on Resurrection Sunday Event at Church.

Karen and I in Montgomery.

Me in my hat.

Me with my Shofar from Israel.

GOD is Good

What I have been doing between 2018 and 2020.

Arab Put
PRAYER
Back In
THE GAME

Arab Put
PRAYER
Back In
THE GAME

Wednesday, Sept. 11, 2019 The Arab Tribune

The Arab Tribune

George pens poem for returning school prayer

Editor:

[illegible]

Stacy Lee George
School Circle
Arab

Wednesday, Oct. 2, 2019 The Arab Tribune

The Arab Tribune

Writer: Time for Arab people to take back PA

Editor:

[illegible]

Stacy Lee George
Arab
[illegible]

Arab Let the Children Pray on the PA!

by Stacy Lee George

Why can't students at the Arab Football stadium use the PA to pray?
It's simple, the devil took the microphone away;
The Freedom from Religion is an arm of Satan, this we must all realize,
They are crusading as constitutional patriots, but that's just a disguise;
They send bullying letters to schools and a few give in,
Most school leaders trash the letter and say, "let the prayer begin";
Some have weak school superintendents who quickly fall in the trap,
Next, a moment of silence will be in place and it's a wrap;
It's time for the people of Arab to take back their P.A.,
We all know it's not a crime for children to pray;
Other schools pray on the P.A. every game day.

Join us at 8:00 pm nightly until November 1st for a Live Facebook prayer on Stacy Lee George's Facebook page. Questions? Call 256-758-1919

Inspired by the issue of putting student led prayer back in the Arab Football home games.

The P.A. is the best way to let the Children Pray!

by Stacy Lee George

Why have people been praying at football games from day one?
Because it is one of the more dangerous sports under the sun;

Why would a student want to pray before a game on the P.A. and what might they say?
They would be asking for the safety of players and it would end in Jesus name we pray;

Why is it important for a student to use the microphone?
They want everyone to be on the same page in prayer and it is simple, it increases the tone;

Some people say they already pray as a group before the game,
But, without the microphone it is not the same;

Why is it not the same if just a few people pray on the field?
Because when praying for God's protection the larger the number the stronger the shield;

Just let the students pray on the P.A.,
Either way, Freedom from Religion will have something to say;

It doesn't matter how they pray the Freedom from Religion will always be mad,
They are the arm of Satan, as long as someone is praying to GOD, they will always be sad;

Let me ask you a question and this issue will be clear as a bell,
But I will have to take your mind off the football field, but just for a spell;

If the doctor said, "you have 3 days to live so you better pray GOD heals you."
Would you want a thousand people praying in unity or only a few?

Join us at 8:00 pm nightly until Nov. 1st for a Live Facebook prayer on Stacy Lee George's Facebook page. Questions? Call 256-758-1919

Inspired by the issue of putting student led prayer back in the Arab Football home games.

Arab Put
PRAYER
Back In
THE GAME

Arab Put
PRAYER
Back In
THE GAME

In loving memory of my dad
Henry (Snooks) George and my sister
Kristie George Wilson. My mother
Leola and me are the lone
survivors. Stacy Lee George
9/6/21 @ 3:33pm

SUMMARY AND CONCLUSION

After this book is published it is my belief with a high circulation of this book, I believe it will make government more honest wherever this book is read. May GOD BLESS Alabama and GOD BLESS America.

During my time as a Morgan County Commissioner, I worked with a group of individuals in various political positions, and I formed an opinion that certain individuals should be in prison. After my 8 years as a Morgan County Commissioner I went to Selma, AL for 3 months of training including APOST-c certification to become a correctional officer in the largest prison in Alabama (Limestone Prison). During the last 12 years as a seasoned Correctional Officer, I have concluded that there are many people in the Alabama prison that should have already gone home and have done their time. This is where we must ask a question. At what point does punishment become revenge? Punishment should be done by the State of Alabama (justice system). Revenge must be left to GOD. There are some judges in Alabama that are playing GOD and there is only one GOD and GOD is NOT happy. Now, some people should be in prison and should never go home. I say all of this to lead you to this point. I have gone from working with a group of people that should be in prison, to working with a group of people who are in prison that should not be in prison. In the end, technically I ended up in prison myself at least 12 hours a day working as a Correctional Officer. GOD has a strange way of directing our path and it is all one big mystery.

Luke 4:18-19 NKJV

18 "The Spirit of the LORD *is* upon Me,
Because He has anointed Me
To preach the gospel to *the* poor;
He has sent Me [i]to heal the brokenhearted,
To proclaim liberty to *the* captives
And recovery of sight to *the* blind,
To set at liberty those who are [j]oppressed;
19 To proclaim the acceptable year of the LORD."

In the end I leave you with a quote. "If it is done in the dark, it must be brought to the light (made public) and if it survives in the light, it is probably alright." Stacy Lee George

John 1:5 NKJV

And the light shines in the darkness, and the darkness did not comprehend it.

Printed in the United States
by Baker & Taylor Publisher Services